BODYBUILDING 101

BODYBUILDING 101

Everything You Need to Know to Get the Body You Want

Robert Wolff, Ph.D.

CONTEMPORARY BOOKS

Library of Congress Cataloging-in-Publication Data

Wolff, Robert, Ph.D.
    Bodybuilding 101 : everything you need to know to get the body
you want / Robert Wolff ; forewords by Joe Weider, Ben Weider, and
Cory Everson.
       p.   cm.
    ISBN 0-8092-2784-3
    1. Bodybuilding.   I. Title.
GV546.5.W65   1999
646.7′5—dc21   98-34339
                                                    CIP

Cover design by Todd Petersen
Cover photograph copyright © 1995 Robert Reiff, Weider Health/Fitness
Interior design by Hespenheide Design
Interior photographs copyright © Weider Publications, Inc.

Published by Contemporary Books
A division of NTC/Contemporary Publishing Group, Inc.
4255 West Touhy Avenue, Lincolnwood (Chicago), Illinois 60712-1975 U.S.A.
Copyright © 1999 by The Creative Syndicate, Inc.
Printed in the United States of America
International Standard Book Number: 0-8092-2784-3

5 6 7 8 9 0 VLP VLP 0 5 4 3 2 1

CONTENTS

FOREWORD

By Joe Weider

In the 60-plus years that I've dedicated my life to bodybuilding, health, and fitness, I've seen many incredible transformations. Men who were skinny all their lives now have more muscle; women who were always overweight and out of shape now have sleek and beautiful bodies; older men and women who were constantly tired and prone to injury and disease are now revitalized, energized, strengthened, and full of new confidence and power. All of these changes can be linked, at least in part, to bodybuilding.

In those same 60-plus years, I've sought out and worked with the world's best bodybuilders, photographers, and writers. And of all the writers who have written for my magazines, one of the best—a man who has changed lives through bodybuilding and motivation—is Robert Wolff.

A good writer leaves a good impression in the reader's mind; a great writer changes people's lives. Robert Wolff is such a writer. Unlike so many others, Robert lives what he preaches—he's in the gym, training hard, always looking for new ways to train more effectively. He's never forgotten what it's like to be a beginner and to be the one who has questions that desperately need right answers. Robert Wolff has

the uncanny ability to discover the subtleties that turn a good exercise into a great one, and then cut through the hype and explain it to the average person in easy and motivational ways he or she can understand and remember.

The book you're now holding came about as an idea Robert discussed with me shortly after he moved to California to write for me full time. I saw great potential in him, his passion for the sport, and his ideas; and I must say, he has always proved me right. In the years that Robert created and wrote the "Bodybuilding 101" column for *Muscle & Fitness* magazine, it was a reader favorite month after month after month.

Why was it such an instant success? I believe Robert spoke to our readers in a way they understood. His powerful motivational style gave readers only the stuff that worked. He gave them information, ideas, motivation, and inspiration they weren't getting from any other writer or magazine. They responded with letter after letter telling just how much his words and bodybuilding changed their lives.

I'm proud to give you *Bodybuilding 101*. What you're about to read will change your life. Enjoy, and best of luck to you!

FOREWORD

By Ben Weider, C.M., Ph.D.

President, International Federation of Bodybuilders

As president of the International Federation of Bodybuilders (IFBB), bodybuilding's international governing organization (in 169 countries), I've been able to travel to over 100 countries all over the world and witness firsthand the incredible effects bodybuilding has on people's lives. From Russia to Mexico, from China to Australia, and in all other countries in-between, the sport of bodybuilding has not only built bodies, but improved lives and nations as well.

Bodybuilding is powerful. It has the ability to transform, to bring out the very best in human potential of every man and woman on this planet. Like any sport, the key to getting the most from it is to first know how to use it correctly. And there is no one who can teach you better than Robert Wolff.

It's one thing for someone to show people how to exercise; it's quite a rarity for someone to be able to motivate and inspire you to *want* to exercise and change your life. Robert Wolff can.

I know for a fact just how hugely successful his "Bodybuilding 101" column was for *Muscle & Fitness* magazine, because all over the world, people told me just how much it changed their lives. Many times, I would ask them, Why?

People say Robert speaks to them in the ways they understand best, giving them information that is tested and refined to work incredibly well for anyone, regardless of age, sex, experience, or where one lives.

This is very important—because for any sport to be accepted and embraced by people, that sport must work for anyone, anywhere, anytime, and give people predictable and consistent results. Everything you're about to read in *Bodybuilding 101* will give you that and much, much more.

The key to getting the most from this book is to use it. *Do it now!* has always been my credo, for we change our lives and the world by taking action instead of simply thinking about it. So if you're that person who wants to make those changes, you couldn't find a better book or person to inspire you and teach you.

With great pleasure I give you the life-changing message of bodybuilding, from *Bodybuilding 101*. Listen to Robert Wolff. The world over, he has proved he's the one who knows how to do it! Warmest wishes for your success.

FOREWORD

By Cory Everson
Six-time Ms. Olympia

The day my life changed was the day I picked up my first weight. Never before had I felt such an incredible sensation all over my body! From that day on, I would never stop. Bodybuilding opened a whole new world for me and allowed me to win the title of best female bodybuilder in the world—Ms. Olympia—six times. The sport also opened doors to movies, books, my own television show on ESPN, and so much more.

But for the majority of us, bodybuilding will never be about winning titles, trophies, or acting. It's about looking and feeling your best. It's about changing your life. And the guy who can inspire, motivate, and show you how to do it like no other is my friend, Robert Wolff.

His book, *Bodybuilding 101*, and his message contain only the best of the best about what you must know to have the body you've always wanted and to look and feel your absolute best. No other kind of physical activity can change your body more quickly than bodybuilding. And no other writer and book can give you the priceless jewels of training wisdom learned from years of workouts and working alongside the greatest names in the sport like Robert Wolff and *Bodybuilding 101*. As you'll soon see and feel, it's the best way of life.

But I caution you not to fall victim to the thinking that holds back many people who exercise: the idea that in order for something to work great, it needs to be complicated. Nothing could be further from the truth. Bodybuilding, real bodybuilding, is pure, powerful, and so incredibly simple. Remember, it's not about shape, it's about figures; as in watching those figures, like keeping cholesterol down, fat intake low, and complex carbs and protein up. All these things will give you a great figure!

This is a very exciting time for the sport of bodybuilding, and you couldn't have picked a better time to be a part of this great sport. Bodybuilding is now recognized as an Olympic sport by the International Olympic Committee, and this is great news for all of us. I predict that in the upcoming years, we'll see an explosion in the popularity of bodybuilding—more than in the 24 years it took me to win my six Ms. Olympia titles—along with more breakthroughs in the science of nutrition and training. All these things will benefit you.

Yet the one thing that will not change is the foundational basics you must know and do before you can build the body you've always wanted but never knew how to achieve. The book you are now holding, *Bodybuilding 101*, will be the guide you'll refer to time and time again, because Robert Wolff's message and inspiration are timeless—and I guarantee they will work wonders for you if you follow his advice. And all you have to do is the same thing we all did . . . get started! Best wishes to you!

I like simple things, so I give you this:

- Enjoy yourself, have fun, and read this book at your own pace. Don't feel pressured to read all of it this week or even this month. This is a book you'll keep for a long time. It's going to be your road map and a constant reference that you'll want to return to time and time again for inspiration and motivation and to answer any questions that may come to you in the future.

- Build a strong foundation first, and whatever house you want to put on top of it will stand for the rest of your life without needing repair. I'm talking about building your body brick-by-brick; everything you're about to learn will be a brick that all other bricks will rest upon. I know you want to get to the cool stuff right away, but take time to build the foundation and set the grooves (which you'll soon learn), and you will look great and be injury-free for life! No exceptions to this rule—you hear me? None!

- Once the foundation is built—that is, once you've built that foundation by training your body with the basics—have fun and do any kind of workout you feel inspired to do. The days of feeling like you have to work out three or more days a week are over. Stop the guilt right now. No one can tell you or give what you want and need except yourself. Listen to your intuition, for it will tell you which body parts and exer-

cises you should do that day and when you should train again.

- Do only the exercises you want to do, when you want to do them. Forget schedules. You're the only one who lives your life, and you're the only one who has your body, dreams, and goals—and when and how you train should reflect that. Training according to your instincts will keep you constantly inspired, motivated, and looking forward—big time!—to your next workout.

- Be your own best buddy. Life is tough enough. Make the gym and your workouts your own special time that nothing and no one will take away from you—ever! It's your gift that you give to yourself for yourself, to make you look and feel great. Yeah, go ahead and be selfish. You deserve it.

- Take it slow. Forget about having that ideal body this month or next. Enjoy the road trip. Believe me, you're going to reach your destination soon enough. Have fun and soak up the sights, experiences, and lessons along the way, because I can promise you this: once you reach your goal, you'll be satisfied for only a short time before you'll want to start on the next road to a new goal. My friend, that's just the way life is.

- Don't compare! I want you to think about something: ever notice how bad or inadequate you feel when you compare your body, your life, or whatever to someone else? Comparison is one of the greatest causes of unhappiness in our lives, so don't do it. Set your own standard for what you want to achieve and experience—and never use anyone else's criteria for how you should look or feel—and you'll be amazed at how much pressure you'll immediately take off yourself and how much more enjoyable everything about your life will instantly become!

ACKNOWLEDGMENTS

No book is ever written alone, and this one is no exception. First of all, I wish to thank Joe and Ben Weider for all their support and belief in me, the opportunities they've given me, and their inspiration and vision that they never gave up despite obstacles and hardship.

I'd like to thank all my friends at *Muscle & Fitness* magazine. Thank you for the opportunities you gave me and all the wonderful experiences. I'll always cherish working with such great people.

I want to thank all the people at Weider Health & Fitness, especially Bernard Cartoon, Ron Novak, Ali Rashid, Eric Weider and Michael Carr, Anneliese Leyk, and Peggy Sukawaty.

Special thanks to Lisa Clark, Eric Donald, and the photographic brilliance of Robert "I can do it all" Reiff, Ralph "Bodybuilding's hardest-working photographer" DeHaan, and Chris "Magic" Lund. You guys are the best!

Thank you to all my friends in the sport of bodybuilding. From bodybuilding and fitness athletes and champions, writers, coaches, photographers, scientists, researchers, doctors, health and fitness experts, and everyone in-between—your passion, commitment, desire, and friendship have been truly inspiring.

A very special thank you to Rachel McLish, Steve Reeves, Lee Haney, and Cory Everson.

Many thanks to the one and only Dr. James E. Wright.

Thank you Matthew Carnicelli, Jenna DiGregorio, Craig Bolt, and everyone at Contemporary Books for your support and great job on this project and the many others to come.

A very special thank you to John and Terri Little for your great friendship, advice, and inspiration. Many thanks to Pete Sisco.

Of course, a big thank you to all my family and friends for your love and belief. I cherish each and every one of you always. Yes, especially you, Mom!

Finally, I thank God for blessing my life with the talents I have and giving me the passion and desire to help others by writing and communicating in ways that people seem to understand. Thank you for helping me understand that we are all brothers and sisters on this earth and that anything we can do to help one person ripples in this great sea of life and automatically helps so many others.

And thank you, my new friend who is now reading this book. Get ready, because your life is about to be changed forever!

INTRODUCTION

Unleashing the Greatness Within You

We all want to be inspired, don't we? We all want to change our lives, whether we actually believe we can or not. And we all want to feel good, look and act young, be vibrant and full of energy and life—to be able do the things we want to do whenever and wherever we want to do them. No limits!

Yes, something inside each of us seems to desire that so strongly. We want to grow. And you know something? This is good, for the law of nature is that you are either growing or you are dying. There's no in-between.

My road to unleashing the greatness within me began once I touched the iron for the first time. An incredibly powerful connection was made between the unbendable iron and an unbendable will that would not let me accept anything but the very best I was capable of. I want to be able to give something my all, and at the end of the day be able to look myself in the mirror and say, "Yeah, I did my best today, and tomorrow I'll do just a little bit better."

But I'm not alone, and I never was. For such great and inspiring people as Arnold Schwarzenegger, Steve Reeves, and so many others all felt the same calling, each in a unique way.

For those who have never touched a weight, all of this must sound like fantasy: "I mean, come on—you're telling me that lifting iron and bodybuilding have that much power to unleash the greatness in anyone?" That's exactly what I'm telling you!

Fortunately for you, me, and the rest of the world, two men from Canada were touched in the same way many years ago. What they've done to create a new and healthier way of life and change countless millions of people's lives in the process is nothing short of astonishing. Their names are Joe and Ben Weider.

Joe and Ben began with a dream to spread the word about the incredible life-changing benefits of bodybuilding to anyone who would listen. Years ago, very few did listen. Now, people can't seem to get enough of that message.

Joe went on to work with the best bodybuilding champions the sport has ever known, and created such top-quality magazines as *Muscle & Fitness*, *Shape*, *Men's Fitness*, *Flex*, and many others. These all have inspired and helped men and women all over the world lead healthier, happier, and more enriched lives by giving them the tools to create whatever body and level of fitness they desire.

Ben devoted his life to spreading the word about bodybuilding to as many people around the world as possible by creating the International Federation of Bodybuilders (IFBB), one of the world's largest and most respected international sports federations for bodybuilding and bodybuilders.

The lifelong work of Ben Weider has not gone unnoticed, despite all the naysayers who merely laughed at his efforts as a futile waste of time. It seems Ben has had the last laugh. The

IFBB is now one of the largest and most powerful sports federations—of any sport—in the world, with over 169 member nations and millions of participants. The IFBB has now been awarded Olympic recognition by the International Olympic Committee. This is truly a milestone, for Ben Weider's work has opened the doors so that bodybuilders from all over the world can now be considered on the same level as other athletes. Not only that, Olympic recognition also means that millions of people will be able to see bodybuilding on television and become inspired to take up this wonderful sport.

So why is all of this important to you, you may ask? Because what you're about to read will change your life. I guarantee it, because it's written just for you with only the stuff that works.

What you're about to read has stood the test of time from people all over the world, just like you, who want real-world information for real-world people, without the hype. With this book, I'm going to inspire you to believe in your greatness, just as Joe and Ben Weider did for me with their magazines and life-changing message.

Never underestimate the power of bodybuilding to change the way you look, the way you feel, and your life in general. You are holding in your hands the most powerfully effective ways to get the maximum out of bodybuilding. Think of it like this: you've just been given a toolbox with all the tools you'll need to transform yourself and unleash the greatness inside of you. All you have to do is use them.

Even though we may have never met face-to-face, I believe in your greatness. Because whoever you may be, wherever you may live, and whatever you may look like, you have the desire and the power inside you to become everything you ever dreamed of and much, much more!

Forget the past and what you could have done or should have done. It doesn't matter. Right now is your new beginning, a fresh start, a clean slate that has nothing written on it at all. You're about to finally achieve the kind of life and look you've always wanted.

Welcome, my friend. You've arrived on the road in your life where incredible things are about to happen—and this book and bodybuilding will help you accomplish them!

BODYBUILDING
101

PART I

In the Beginning . . .

What You Should Know About Beginning Bodybuilding

From Reps to Weights to the Number of Days You Should Train

I remember the first time I picked up *Muscle & Fitness* magazine. As a rank beginner, I was hungry for anything I could learn about bodybuilding and nutrition. The magazines didn't come out quickly enough to satisfy my appetite.

Yet after a short time, the more I read, the more confused I became. Each expert and pro bodybuilder had his or her own unique style of training and philosophy. Each was the gospel—and with so many gospels, which one was I supposed to believe? I began to feel frustrated!

Then the light came on. I realized that every pro and expert had merely found what worked best for himself or herself. In essence, each took from a huge pool of training routines, exercises, set-and-rep combinations, and theories only those things that worked best for himself or herself. From that pool of knowledge, I would have to extract those elements that would work best for *me*, given *my* genetic potential and personal goals.

Of course, reading the book you now have in your hands will really

help you see the big picture when it comes to understanding your body. Having a solid understanding of all the elements of bodybuilding will help you apply important principles to your fitness program right now. Let's get started.

THE ABCs OF HOW TO BEGIN

First of all, let's define a *beginner*. A beginner either has never lifted weights before, may have lifted years ago but stopped, or hasn't trained on a regular basis for over six months.

When does a beginner become an intermediate and move on to a new training program? One school of thought says that a beginner should use a combination of machines, cables, and freeweight exercises, including supersets and forced reps, to get better workouts. Proponents of this system agree that a beginner is only a beginner until he can handle more weight, then he graduates to the intermediate level. I don't belong to this school of thought.

I believe, like many others, that a beginner should not rush through a beginner program. Developing a solid foundation—using basic exercises and excellent form—will help ensure a lifetime of injury-free training. *This is very important* and should be the first and foremost goal of any serious beginner.

Many of today's top bodybuilders once used this method as beginners and stayed on the system for almost a full year. Results speak for themselves. I know firsthand. I trained on this beginner's program for the first two years of my training and gained 65 pounds of muscle—drug-free! Moreover, after 20 years of training, I have not had a single injury. The same can happen for you. Building a solid foundation is the answer.

I am amazed at what I see in the gyms today. Many times, I see beginning bodybuilders doing *finishing movements* (like dumbbell concentration curls for 12-inch arms!) when they don't even have much mass to finish or shape. I want to ask them, "Hey, what are you doing, shaping the bone?"

Some of the most common injuries among beginners result from doing too much too soon. As a beginner, one of the most difficult things you'll ever face is holding yourself back from adding those extra exercises, sets, reps, and plates before your body is ready for them.

Because beginners often make good gains very quickly, many fall into the trap of thinking more is better. This is true later in the training equation, but not for a novice. Let me tell you right now, stick with the basics that will build a rock-solid foundation, and don't overtrain.

UNDERSTANDING BODYBUILDING JARGON

Bodybuilding, like other sports, has its own rules and vocabulary. Getting to know the lingo will help you better understand and enjoy this great sport. Here is a basic vocabulary lesson for the beginner.

Aerobic—Exercise that primarily uses oxygen to burn fuel at low to moderate levels of intensity.

Anaerobic—Exercise that primarily uses the body's stored fuel (glycogen and phosphocreatine) for energy. Intense weightlifting is an anaerobic exercise.

Cardiovascular—Referring to the heart, lungs, and other periphery systems involved in the transport of oxygen throughout the body.

Intensity—The degree to which the body is worked during exercise. There are two types:

- Absolute intensity—The percentage of one-rep max you are working.

- Relative intensity—Relative level of effort. For example, if you use 65 percent of your one-rep max (low to moderate absolute intensity), and you do as many reps as you can, this is a very high degree of relative intensity.

Overload—Process by which specific muscles are worked beyond their normal capacity of strength and/or endurance.

Progressive resistance—The principle of continually adding more weight on a specific exercise as your muscles become stronger and adapt to the heavier weights.

Rep—One execution of any exercise.

Routine—The specific exercises, weights, sets, and reps for a specific body part.

Set—A combination of any number of reps of one exercise.

Workout—The routine, specific exercises, weights, sets, and reps for one or more body parts.

TRAIN BIG MUSCLES FIRST

Remember this rule of thumb: Train your big muscle groups first. That means hitting legs, back, and chest before training shoulders and arms. Here's why.

Larger muscle groups demand more energy and intensity to make them grow and get stronger than do smaller muscle groups. If you train arms with all-out intensity and then do chest immediately afterward, you won't have enough energy to generate the training intensity necessary to stimulate growth. Moreover, because the triceps are required in chest movements, your arms will fail much more quickly than your chest muscles, which will hold back your chest training.

Also, the metabolic and neurologic demands from training a large muscle group can easily put your body into a state of overtraining (which can lead to decreased strength and energy as well as stalled gains) if you're not careful. That's why it's crucial that you get in the gym, work your body hard, and then get out and rest! The amount of time you spend in the gym is irrelevant; what counts is what you do when you're there! Always train your bigger muscles first when your energy level is greatest.

HOW MUCH WEIGHT SHOULD YOU USE?

This is probably the most common question I get. Of course, I can't answer it for you, because everyone's level of strength is different. Take a little extra time to experiment and find the right weights for all the exercises you do. It won't take long, and it'll be well worth whatever time you spend. Here's how you can do it.

Let's say you're doing an incline barbell bench press for chest. With just the bar, press the weight up and down. Easy, isn't it? Now take two 10-pound weights and place one on each end of the bar. Again, press the weight up and down, but this time do 10 reps. Was it easy? If it was really easy, add another 10-pounder (or "dime") on each side and do another 10 reps. If it wasn't so easy, try adding a $2^1/2$- or 5-pound plate on each side. Continue this process until it becomes tough to complete 8 to 10 reps. Once you can lift a weight for 10 reps, increase it by approximately 10 percent.

Of course, never sacrifice excellent form just for the sake of lifting heavier weights. The reality is, you need to overload your muscles with progressively heavier weight if you want them to grow and become stronger. But always keep in mind that in bodybuilding, weight is only a means to an end and never an end itself. I've seen many of the world's best pro bodybuilders take a light weight and make it feel heavy, achieving great results. Making the muscle work hard with proper form is the name of the game!

BREATHING AND PROPER FORM

Most of us breathe without thinking about it. But proper workout form demands that you breathe correctly. Here's how to breathe for any exercise you do.

Take a deep breath before you start. When you reach the bottom position of each movement (which is often where the most difficult portion of the movement begins), begin breathing out in a controlled manner until you reach the top position. Remember to inhale at the top or easiest part of the exercise, and exhale throughout the exertion or hardest part of the movement.

THE IMPORTANCE OF NONTRAINING DAYS

Let's talk a little about days off. As a beginner, you're going to be brimming with enthusiasm for working out. After all, this is a new sport that promises to make your body look and feel great. But just as too little exercise won't stimulate your muscles to grow, too much won't either. It's much better for you to not do enough than to do too much.

Most beginners achieve growth spurts unparalleled by more advanced bodybuilders; their bodies seem to grow overnight. Many beginners are also resistant to overtraining—they can push themselves into what would nor-

mally be the overtraining zone, and their bodies will adapt to those demands by growing and getting stronger very quickly.

If only it could last! But it doesn't. Soon the phenomenal growth rate slows down, and the beginning bodybuilder enters the more-intensity-for-any-growth zone. That's why you need to give your body plenty of rest—especially if it's still sore from the last workout—to keep it fresh and growing. *Never train a body part that's still sore from your last workout.* By all means, stretch out and get blood flowing into the sore muscle area, but don't train that body part until it has fully recovered.

Follow your beginner program to the letter, and don't throw in an extra

day of training just because you want your body to grow more rapidly. It won't. If you're on a Monday–Wednesday–Friday program, take those remaining four days off for rest. And *take one week off from working out for every six to eight weeks of consistent training.*

MUSCLE SORENESS: A BODYBUILDER'S BEST FRIEND?

If you're a beginner, one thing can be said with certainty: if you work out, you're going to get sore. Is soreness bad? Not necessarily. The majority of muscle soreness comes from microtears in the muscle fibers, the result of intense exercise. The body repairs these microtears very quickly.

Not only that, but the body also overcompensates during this recovery by making the muscles stronger, thus making it harder for microtearing to occur in the future. Hence, if you're wanting to continue to grow and get stronger, you're going to have to progressively overload your muscles on a regular basis in future workouts.

Progressive overload is the cornerstone of bodybuilding success.

Muscle soreness can become a problem when the body is pushed too hard too fast. Use of high-intensity training principles like those used by

more advanced bodybuilders—such as supersets, tri-sets, forced reps, drop sets, rest–pause, and negatives—can put the skids on a beginner's progress. The joints, tendons, and ligaments of a beginner haven't yet strengthened sufficiently to sustain these kinds of workouts to get the full benefit and intended results that these intermediate/advanced principles offer.

Use muscle soreness as a gauge to measure workout intensity and effectiveness. Soreness can be a good thing if not taken to extremes. However, most pros will tell you that you don't need to get sore after every workout to grow and get stronger.

YOUR CHANGING NUTRITIONAL NEEDS

Most beginners are interested in one thing—getting massive. Even if their training is right on target, if they neglect one crucial component—diet—they can kiss their dreams of big muscles goodbye.

So, how's your diet? It should include the following:

- Four to six small meals per day.
- 50 percent calories from carbs, 35 percent from protein, and 15 percent from fat.
- A carb-replacement drink with 50 to 75 grams of carbs within 30 minutes after each workout. (A 12- to 16-ounce bottle of fruit juice works great.)
- About 40 to 55 grams of protein within 90 minutes after working out.

If you're missing any of these elements, then your diet is holding you back from maximizing bodybuilding gains. All of these are sound nutritional strategies that will give you a head start on building muscle mass while keeping body-fat levels low.

What Should You Eat?

Let me give you a few recommendations. For protein, stick with lean sources like beef (I recommend flank steak), skinless chicken and turkey, eggwhites, and a whey- or egg-based protein powder. You have a number of choices when it comes to carbohydrates. For sustained energy, the complex carbs such as vegetables, rice, whole grains, and pasta work well. Simple carbs, including strawberries, melons, bananas, apples, and grapefruit, provide quick energy but should be eaten in moderation.

If eating four to six balanced meals each day is difficult, substitute a protein shake for one or two of your regular meals. These are ideal for anyone who has a busy schedule. I also strongly suggest that you have a protein shake or protein meal about 90 minutes before bedtime. I found that as a hard-training beginning bodybuilder, my body was in a near-constant state of hunger. I also discovered that the only thing that would keep my stomach from growling at night was a high-protein meal about 90 minutes or so before bedtime. Eating my final meal at 6 or 7 P.M. and then waiting a full 12 hours before breakfast left me feeling weak, flat, and lethargic. The extra late-night protein meal was the perfect answer. Make sure, however, that you don't eat too close to bedtime.

WHEN TO CHANGE YOUR WORKOUT

Often, a bodybuilder will find a routine and stick with it—not because it works (though it may have been great at one time), but because it's comfortable, and change requires thought. But changing your routine not only signifies a jump to a higher level (for example, from beginner to intermediate) but also stimulates your muscles in new, growth-creating ways.

GETTING READY FOR INTERMEDIATE TRAINING

- Identify your goals. Do you want to gain muscle mass? Lose body fat? Maintain the muscles you have and improve definition? Decide exactly what you want.

- If your goal is more muscle mass, then focus your attention on barbell and dumbbell movements, using heavier weights and a slightly longer rest time between sets.

- If your goal is to lose body fat and gain muscle definition, then focus your attention on dumbbells, machines, and cables. Pick up the pace, take shorter rest periods between sets, use lighter weights, and do more reps.

- From a wide variety of exercises for each body part, *create at least five whole-body workouts and do two to three different exercises for each body part every training day.*

The exercises should make use of the categories I've just mentioned (barbells, dumbbells, machines, and cables) that conform to your goals.

- In a journal, write down every exercise you do, noting how each felt. (See page 50 for more on keeping a training log.) Did you get a great pump? Did you get sore? If so, how sore and for how many days? Did it make your muscles burn? Think of as many ways as possible to judge each exercise you do.

- *Throw out the ineffective exercises and keep only those your body responds to best.* Find at least five excellent exercises for each body part, and use two to three of them per body part, each workout. On the next workout, change the exercises.

- Constantly change the exercises, order performed, tempo of training, reps, weight, angles, and rest between reps and sets.

You've got to keep your body off-guard if you want it to grow, get stronger, and be in better shape!

When to change your training, however, cannot be generalized; genetics, training goals, previous experience, desire, existing level of strength, and growth development are all major factors that must be considered before moving to the next level.

As a rule, stay on your beginner program for at least four months. Training longer at this level certainly will not hurt you! During those four months, you should have developed excellent exercise form and have found your body's own exercise groove using the basic movements, strengthened your muscles and connective tissue, and established the all-important mind–muscle link for increased intensity and greater results.

Once you become an intermediate, you'll notice a number of changes: working out more frequently with more sets and heavier weights, using high-intensity training principles, increasing nutrient uptake and supplementation, and needing more rest.

Most likely, you will want to add *a few* shaping movements, like dumbbell side laterals for the delts, to your routine. For someone wanting to gain muscle mass, the emphasis on his or her training should be 90 percent compound movements, that is, multijoint exercises that build size and strength, like squats and rows, and 10 percent isolation–shaping movements, that is, single joint exercises, like dumbbell concentration curls for biceps peak. Remember, you've got to have the size before you start chiseling your body!

THE BEGINNER'S WORKOUT

One of the best beginner programs is the three-days-a-week routine. For example, do a whole-body workout on Monday, Wednesday, and Friday—the other days are for rest. Begin your workout with your legs, your biggest muscle group. Here's the routine:

Exercise	Sets	Reps
Legs		
Leg extension (warm-up)	2	15
Squat	2	8
Leg curl	2	10
Standing calf raise	2	10–15
Chest		
Incline bench press (using only the bar and no extra weight—warm-up)	1–2	12–20
Incline barbell bench press	2	8
Flat bench dumbbell flye	2	8–10
Back		
Chin-up *or*	2	8–10
pulldown	2	10–15
Bent-over row	2	6–10
Shoulders		
Seated overhead press (barbell or dumbbell)	2	8–10
Upright row	2	10–15
Biceps		
Standing barbell curl	2	5–9
Triceps		
Dip *or*	2	limit
pressdown	2	10–15
Abdominals		
Crunch	2	20–30

Leg extension

Incline barbell bench press

Pulldown

Seated overhead press

Standing barbell curl

Pressdown

Crunch

BUILDING THE FOUNDATION

The greatest physiques of yesterday and today were developed through basic exercises. Here's a list of some of the best:

- **Chest**—Bench press, incline press, dip, flye
- **Back**—Chin-up, deadlift, T-bar row, one-arm dumbbell row, bent-over row, seated row, pulldown
- **Quads**—Squat, hack squat, leg press
- **Hamstrings**—Stiff-legged deadlift, leg curl
- **Calves**—Calf raise (standing, seated, and donkey)
- **Shoulders**—Barbell and dumbbell overhead press, dumbbell side lateral
- **Trapezius**—Shrug, upright row
- **Biceps**—Standing barbell curl, alternate dumbbell curl
- **Triceps**—Dip, close-grip bench press, French press (overhead or lying), pressdown
- **Abdominals**—Reverse crunch, crunch

> "He who gains victory over other men is strong; but he who gains a victory over himself is all-powerful."
>
> —Lao-tzu

Many times in life, you are faced with tough decisions—and in those times, it helps to know which decisions are important to make and which ones aren't. Resist the temptation—either in the gym or out of it—to live your life just trying to be better than someone else. The person you are competing against probably couldn't care less, and the world only cares if *you* are the best *you* can be. Never try to be a copy of someone else, because you never will be. Just realizing that will save you untold years of heartache and frustration. Use the iron to teach you ways to overcome your self-imposed limitations, and you'll be on the right path to becoming the very best you can be.

2

The Basics of Nutrition and Supplements

What You're About to Learn Will Change Your Body and Your Life!

Proper nutrition is responsible for at least 50 percent of your success as a bodybuilder. Of course, you've got to train vigorously and intelligently and get enough rest, but don't make the mistake of underestimating the role that proper nutrition plays in how your body looks and feels.

Think about it. When you say you want to get bigger or lose weight, you're actually trying to control the way food is affecting your body's appearance and function, aren't you? While working out is a big factor, food is even more important.

NUTRITION GUIDELINES– HOW TO EAT

Knowing which foods to eat, when to eat them, how much to eat, and what to drink is absolutely essential to your bodybuilding and fitness success! Here are some guidelines to follow.

1. Eat four to six small meals a day, about three hours apart. Small meals are more easily digested and result in greater nutrient absorption. This

helps ensure that your body will more efficiently use the nutrients you feed it.

2. Remember the one-half/one-third rule—fill one-half of your plate with carbohydrates and the remaining one-third with protein. These ideal food proportions ensure that you're getting about 50 percent of your calories from carbs, 35 percent from protein, and the remaining 15 percent from fats.

3. Choose your foods carefully. Try getting your carbohydrates from sources such as rice, vegetables, beans, lentils, whole grains, pasta, and fruit. Good protein sources include fish, chicken, turkey, lean meat, and low-fat or nonfat dairy products. Don't be concerned with adding fats to your diet; instead, pay attention to minimizing your dietary fat intake. Eating foods with too much fat causes your body's appearance to change—and not for the better.

4. Drink a *minimum* of 10 eight-ounce glasses of water each day. Don't try drinking them all at once, especially during a meal, as water tends to neutralize body enzymes that are used for food breakdown and digestion. Drink all the water you want about 10 to 15 minutes before your meal, and then only sip while eating. This will allow the water to be absorbed with minimal dilution of the digestive enzymes.

You may worry that drinking too much water will bloat you—but in fact, just the opposite happens. When the body isn't given enough water, it tends to hold the fluids it has until more is ingested. Giving your body enough fluid throughout the whole day tells the body that there's no need to worry—more will be coming soon.

5. The best time to replenish your muscle glycogen stores with carbs is immediately following your workout, when the body has increased ability to effectively store carbs. Get 50 to 75 grams of carbs into your body right after the workout by drinking a can of fruit juice or a carb-replacement drink.

6. Timing your protein intake right after a workout is also crucial to getting a jump start on muscle growth and repair. About 75 minutes (give or take a few minutes) after your workout is a great time to give your body a pro-

tein meal. Try to eat at least 40 to 55 grams of high-quality protein, and you'll be way ahead in building muscle and strength.

7. Make a conscious effort to avoid eating junk food and fast food. Once in a while is okay—after all, you gotta have fun, right? The problem comes when you eat them too often. While these foods are convenient and tasty, they can definitely wreak havoc on your body's appearance and function. These foods are loaded with all kinds of fats, sodium, refined sugars, preservatives, and other things that won't contribute one iota to your bodybuilding and fitness success.

Changing your eating habits takes discipline. Yet it's easier than you might think once you realize how eating properly will make you look and feel.

The champions know that proper nutrition is essential to their success. You'll know it, too, once you begin eating like the champion you know you can be. Follow the simple guidelines I've just given, and I know you will look and feel great!

EATING TO LOSE

If you want to lose body fat and build muscle at the same time, you've got to cut calories without adversely affecting the rest of your nutritional game plan. And that means you've got to find out just how many calories you should be eating based on your metabolism.

Don't worry, it's much easier than you think. One of the simplest ways to determine how many calories you should eat in a day is to multiply your desired body weight by the number 10, 11, or 12 (10 for a slow metabolism, 11 for a medium metabolism, and 12 for a fast metabolism). If you're one of the fortunate ones who have only a little body fat to lose, try multiplying your desired body weight by 13 or 14 and see how that works. I'll give you two scenarios showing how to use this formula—one for men and one for women.

A Man Who Wants to Weigh 175 Pounds

Target body weight of 175 pounds × 10 (for a slow metabolism) = 1,750 calories per day

1,750 × 50% carbs = 875 calories (218 grams) carbohydrate per day

1,750 × 35% protein = 612.5 calories (153 grams) protein per day

1,750 × 15% fat = 262.5 calories (29 grams) fat per day

A Woman Who Wants to Weigh 136 Pounds

Target body weight 136 pounds × 10 (for a slow metabolism) = 1,360 calories per day

1,360 × 50% carbs = 680 calories (170 grams) carbohydrate per day

1,360 × 35% protein = 476 calories (119 grams) protein per day

1,360 × 15% fat = 204 calories (22 grams) fat per day

As you read earlier, get 50 percent of your calories from carbs, 35 percent from protein, and 15 percent from fats, and you'll be doing fine. Always remember that just one gram of fat has nine calories, whereas a gram from protein or carbohydrate has only four calories. Keep that in mind the next time you've got a major craving for fatty foods!

THE HOW, WHAT, AND WHY OF PROPER SUPPLEMENTATION

Walk into any health-food store, and what do you see? Shelf after shelf of nutritional supplements, all designed to help you look and feel better. But which supplements should you take? Do you really need them? Why should you take them and how much should you take?

First and foremost, you don't want to waste your time and money on supplements that will give you only a little bang for your buck. Out of your supplement dollar, figure 30 cents for vitamins and minerals; 30 cents for protein; 20 cents for a carb-replacement drink; and the remaining 20 cents for amino acids.

The essence of a supplement is just that—a *supplement* to an already good diet. Supplements are not to be used to replace the foods in your diet. While eating healthy and nutritious foods will give you many of the vitamins, minerals, trace elements, protein, carbs, and amino acids you need, your nutritional demands as a bodybuilder are greater than average, and therefore you should consider supplementation.

Many foods lose a great deal of their nutritional value due to processing, preservatives, packaging, and cooking. Meanwhile, bodybuilding places additional nutritional demands on your body, as do such factors as stress, emotions, and hormones.

As a bodybuilder, you should be concerned with supplementing your diet with nutritional products that will support your growth and recuperative needs. Some of these supplements are discussed in the following section.

Vitamins and Minerals

Vitamins and minerals are necessary for normal body function and repair. These metabolic spark plugs help convert the foods you eat into energy. Individual vitamins and minerals also perform myriad specialized duties. Many bodybuilders find that taking a multivitamin/mineral supplement every day is an ideal way to get the right combination of the vitamins and minerals they need. Always take them after your meal, not before.

Amino Acids

Amino acids are the building blocks of protein. All of the 50,000 or so different types of proteins found in your body are made from the 20 essential amino acids called *proteogenic amino acids*. Proteogenic simply means "protein-creating." Of the 20 aminos, the adult body can produce all but eight: lysine, leucine, isoleucine, methionine, phenylalanine, threonine, tryptophan, and valine. Since the body can't produce them, these essential amino acids must come from either the food you eat or the supplements you take. The necessary amounts of all 20 aminos must be present at the same time to ensure that your body will make optimal use of the protein you eat for repair, recuperation, and growth. The deficiency of even one essential amino acid in the diet can lead to a lower level of protein synthesis in the body.

Taking an amino supplement can help facilitate protein synthesis for growth, recuperation, and repair. However, the quality of amino acids can vary widely. Pharmaceutical-grade aminos are the most desirable, yet are also the most expensive. These aminos are absorbed and utilized by the body to a much greater degree than nonpharmaceutical-grade aminos. How can you tell which is which? First: as noted, the price will be higher. Second: the color of pharmaceutical-grade aminos will be pure white. When you see aminos that are off-white or tan, they probably are of a much lower grade. As a bodybuilder, you should be concerned with three types of amino acids: branched-chain, free-form, and peptide bond.

- **Branched-chain amino acids (BCAAs)**—BCAAs are three of the eight essential amino acids whose primary function is protein synthesis. These three aminos—

leucine, isoleucine, and valine—are vital to muscle growth and recovery. Some research has shown that BCAAS taken within 30 minutes after a workout can help prevent muscle catabolism, the breakdown of muscle tissue, and promote increased levels of protein synthesis.

- **Free-form amino acids**—The term *free-form* simply refers to aminos that are composed of the 20 essential amino acids pooled together without bonds. Free-form aminos help ensure that your body has the complete complement of all the aminos when you need them. These are best taken on an empty stomach 30 minutes before meals to ensure their rapid assimilation into the bloodstream.
- **Peptide bonds**—This refers to the number of aminos bonded or held together. The two types of peptide bonds are dipeptides and tripeptides. *Di* means two aminos bonded together and *tri* means three or more aminos bonded together.

Controversy continues as to which aminos (free-form or peptide bond) are better absorbed and utilized by the body. Many scientists feel that aminos that are bonded—that is, in smaller chains—are more quickly absorbed by the body than those without bonds. Others say it doesn't make much difference.

One thing is clear: no matter which amino acid supplement you choose, capsules are better than tablets and powder is better than capsules. Experiment and pick the best amino combination that will help support your bodybuilding and fitness goals.

Creatine

Creatine is a supplement that some people swear by and others swear off—meaning that it works for some and not so well for others. Creatine enhances

activities where short bursts of energy are needed, such as weightlifting and sprinting.

In some studies, creatine has been shown to help a lifter train longer and harder. However, much longer in-depth studies are needed to determine whether this supplement will stand the test of time as a must-have in your gym bag.

Protein- and Carbohydrate-Replacement Drinks

What about protein- and carbohydrate-replacement drinks? Do they help? Yes, I feel that they will help you reach your bodybuilding goals more quickly.

Protein drinks seem to work well in helping a bodybuilder gain weight, lose weight, or maintain size. It all depends on how you use them. Sometimes preparing four to six meals each day can be difficult. That's why many bodybuilders have a protein drink as a supplement to one of those meals. Protein drinks are an excellent way to ingest extra protein without having to worry about excess fat. A high-quality protein drink can help your body grow and recover quickly.

Not all protein powders are alike. Pick one that contains high PER (protein efficiency ratio) ingredients such as whey, eggwhite, or milk protein. Products made with meat or soy proteins are not utilized by the body nearly as well as those made with whey, milk, and egg. And be careful of ingesting too many calories at one time. Taking in 1,000 calories or more with each drink is a good way to overload your system and spoil your appetite for your regular meals. Use common sense and read the labels!

Carbohydrate-replacement drinks work well before, during, and after a workout. These drinks are an excellent source of carbohydrates for energy and can replenish electrolytes lost during your workout. If taken shortly after your workout, they are also an ideal way to refill those muscle glycogen stores. Try diluting the drink with an equal amount of water to enable your body to use the carbs more effectively.

In Search of the Best Supplement: Use Common Sense

You have probably heard stories about people taking extract of bull testicles or some other gland in hopes of becoming bigger and stronger. But so far, research has not found any muscle-building benefits in such extracts. Same with so many of these other "incredible" supplements that seem to pop up all the time. Let the buyer beware.

My advice is to stay with products that have been tested in the gym as well as the laboratory. Buy your supplements from a reputable manufacturer that has been in the sports nutrition business for many years. And don't be misled by supplements offering the highest quality at unbelievably low prices. They're probably too good to be true. In this business, like most others, you get what you pay for.

The right combination of consistent hard training, eating healthy and nutritious foods, getting proper rest, and keeping your mind focused will help you reach your bodybuilding and fitness objectives quickly.

3

Know Thyself

Your Individual Body Type Should Determine Your Training Focus

As you have discovered, working out makes you feel and look good. You're hitting the weights regularly, and as a result your body is changing—for the better. The basic exercises will help you get on the road to fitness success, but soon you'll reach a point where knowing your body type and how it responds to training will take on new importance. Right now, I'm going to give you a sneak preview of a topic we'll go into in much greater depth later in this book.

The three basic body types are:

- **Endomorph**—Characterized by soft musculature, short neck, round face, wide hips, and an inclination toward heavy fat storage
- **Ectomorph**—Characterized by long arms and legs; short upper torso; long, narrow feet and hands; narrow chest and shoulders; very little fat storage; and long, thin muscles
- **Mesomorph**—Characterized by a large chest, long torso, great strength, and solid musculature

As a rule, nobody has just one particular body type, but rather a combination of all three. But each of us leans toward one of the three types, and knowing how these different body types respond to training and diet will help you reach your bodybuilding goals more quickly. Understanding your body type and its specific training and nutritional demands for growth presents new challenges for you. These challenges require that you have a solid game plan to be successful in your training.

FOR THE ENDOMORPH: HIGH REPS, HIGH SETS

Building muscle mass is generally easier if you're an endomorph. Keeping your fat level low may be more of a challenge. Generally, the endomorph responds well to high-set (12 to 15), high-rep (12 to 20) training that allows for only brief rest between sets. Endomorphs respond well to training no more than four or five days per week, as in a two-on/one-off program.

Aerobic training using stationary bikes, treadmills, stairclimbers, and so forth for at least 20 to 30 minutes per workout should be included in your program. Keeping your caloric intake of protein, carbs, and fats to restricted levels is important, but be careful not to go below your daily nutritional requirements for muscle repair and growth.

FOR THE ECTOMORPH: THE IMPORTANCE OF INTENSITY

If you're an ectomorph, building muscle mass can be quite a challenge indeed. Ectomorphs tend to be lean, and putting on size may seem to take forever if you don't follow a solid game plan. However, with proper guidelines, you can get to your bodybuilding goals quickly. These tips will help:

- Do the basic exercises that emphasize power movements for building mass. Exercises like squats, deadlift, presses, chin-ups, rows, and barbell curls are excellent mass builders.
- Keep your reps in the 6 to 8 range and sets in the 8 to 12 range. Be sure to give your body enough rest between sets so you can continue to lift heavy weights, with good form, to induce muscle-fiber stimulation for growth.
- Your training goal should be less volume and greater intensity. Train no more than three days per week in order to give your body sufficient time for recuperation, repair, and growth. The Monday–Wednesday–Friday workout schedule is ideal.

Nutrition is a big factor in gaining weight and muscle mass for the ectomorph. If you're ectomorphic, be sure to take in extra calories throughout the day. Weight-gain powders and protein drinks complement your overall solid nutritional plan while boosting your caloric intake. Limit outside activities in order to save your energy for building muscle mass.

FOR THE MESOMORPH: BORN FOR BODYBUILDING

You could say that mesomorphs are natural bodybuilders. In spite of their ability to put on muscle, mesomorphs still must devote effort, intensity, and perseverance to their training. Mesomorphs, like endomorphs and ectomorphs, benefit from proper training and nutritional guidelines. Here are a few:

- Using a combination of heavy power movements like squats, deadlifts, rows, and presses and shaping movements such as laterals, pressdowns, dumbbell curls, and extensions can give the mesomorph better muscle quality, proportion, and symmetry.
- Mesomorphs respond well to fairly long workouts (up to 80 minutes) and shorter rest between sets (no longer than 45 to 60 seconds). Staying within the 6 to 10 set and 6 to 12 rep range works well for the mesomorph.
- Working out four days a week, such as the two-on/one-off, seems to give the mesomorph's body enough workout frequency and stimulation for growth.
- A balanced diet is generally good enough for the mesomorph to pack on muscle mass—no need to overload your system with massive amounts of protein or carbs. Eat sensibly and keep the body fat to an acceptable level.

Whatever your predominant body type, remember that you are a combination of all three body types. Formulate your training and nutritional plan accordingly. (More on this in later chapters.)

Stay committed to your training. Learn how your body type responds to various training methods, sets, and reps. Structure your training to your body-type needs, and you'll be successful.

> **"I've never known a man worth his salt who in the long run, deep down in his heart, didn't appreciate the grind, the discipline . . . I firmly believe man's finest hour—this greatest fulfillment to all he holds dear—is that moment when he has worked his heart out in a good cause and lies exhausted on the field of battle—victorious."**
>
> **—Vince Lombardi**

The more disciplined you are, the easier your life will be. The less disciplined you are, the harder your life will be. Never forget that. It takes discipline to get your butt in the gym and work out. It takes discipline to make the foods you eat as nutritious as possible. But when you do those things, like magic, your body starts to change—and amazingly, you begin to look and feel great. It's not some miracle exercise, supplement, or food that did it—it was you. And the way you did it was discipline. And even though it may have been tough at first, when you look back on it, you'll say it was one of the best things you ever did.

4

Understanding the Weider Principles for Beginners

The Evolution of the Classic Rules to Grow By

When Joe Weider came on the body-building scene more than 60 years ago, the iron sport was not like the one we know today. Back then, body-builders had no set of coherent rules and principles for enhancing muscle growth and development. Principles like flushing, pyramiding, progressive overload, and compound, super-, tri-, and giant sets were unheard of. Many bodybuilders trained very hard, yet knew very little about how to maximize their training.

Fortunately, things have changed. Through much trial and error, experimentation, and observation, Joe Weider named and categorized a set of easily understandable and applicable rules to help bodybuilders achieve optimum results. These rules are called the Weider Principles. They are broken down into beginning (for those who have trained 6 to 9 months), intermediate (for those who have trained for 9 to 12 months), and advanced (for those who have trained longer than 12 months). In this chapter, we'll take a look at the Weider Principles for beginners.

BEGINNING PRINCIPLES

Progressive Overload. To increase any level of fitness (size, strength, endurance, and so on), you must make your muscles work harder than they are accustomed to working. You must *progressively overload* them. To gain strength, you must constantly try to handle greater weight. To gain muscle size, you need to not only handle heavy weight but also increase the number of sets and workouts as well. This forms the basis for progressive overload.

Set System. This principle involves doing multiple sets per body part in order to completely exhaust each muscle group and stimulate maximum muscle hypertrophy (growth).

Isolation. Muscles can work in unison or they can work in relative separation from each other. Each muscle or muscle group contributes, in some fashion, to a whole movement, either as an *agonist* (contributes to a desired movement by means of contraction), an *antagonist* (contributes to the *opposite* action of a desired movement), a *stabilizer* (contributes equally to an agonist and antagonist), or a *synergist* (complements the action of an agonist). If you want to maximally shape or build a muscle independently, you must isolate it from the other muscles as best as you can.

Muscle Confusion. By constantly varying the exercises, sets, reps, and angles of motion, you prevent your body from adapting to a specific training routine and becoming stale. This is how you continue to grow mass and get stronger.

5

Gym Shopping and Gym Etiquette

What to Look for in a House of Iron

Searching for the right gym can produce either a happy ending or an unhappy one. For the majority of gym members, the stories are happy—finding the right club has made a big difference in their training success. But others wish they would've kept their money in their pockets. So how can you get the maximum benefit and minimum hassle from your gym search? Here are some tips.

- Look for a gym that has a lot of variety. A well-equipped gym should have plenty of freeweights, Olympic sets, and machines.
- A good gym should have plenty of dumbbells.
- The gym should be well organized; body part sections should be grouped together. You don't want to walk all over the gym looking for weights, a bench, or a machine just so you can do another exercise for the same body part.
- The incline bench should always be of varying width. You should have access to a narrow bench so

you don't have to hold the dumbbells out to avoid hitting the bench. And a bench that's four inches wider than the narrow variety should be available for added support when doing pressing movements. Bench press support should be wide and never narrow, for safety's sake.

- The gym should have a spotter's platform for every bench press or shoulder press bench or seat.
- The gym should have a good platform arrangement (minimum size should be 10 × 10 feet) on the floor for deadlifts, squats, and so on.
- Duplication of heavily used equipment is a must in any serious gym. When you go to the gym to work out, you want to work out, not wait around for people to finish their sets just so you can use the equipment.
- Always be suspicious of any piece of equipment that's not bolted down—it's an accident waiting to happen.

CONDITIONING THE HEART AND LUNGS

A prime consideration in choosing a gym is the quality of its facilities for cardiovascular fitness—the area with stationary bikes, stairclimbers, rowing machines, and treadmills. Many people think of these things purely as aerobic equipment, but I think of them differently. Done correctly, a tough workout on a bike can pump up the legs so incredibly that it will feel like you've done an hour of heavy squats! The benefits you'll reap from this type of workout can be tremendous.

PERSONAL TRAINING

A good gym should be well stocked, not only in equipment but in know-how. A gym's instructors should be able to show you how to properly use equipment, and explain the whys and hows of proper breathing; why you should warm up at a certain time and stretch in another; the best sequence for working specific body parts; and so on. A personal instructor should not only know how to train, but should also have knowledge of kinesiology.

RULES

A good gym will have strict rules all members must abide by. These rules ensure that the weights will always be in their proper places, the equipment will stay in good condition, and safety is always paramount.

My friend, I'm sorry to say that far too many clubs let their members run the show, and rarely enforce the rules—if they have them!—strictly enough. Rules can and will benefit every member in the club.

MAINTENANCE AND CLEANLINESS

The gym should be spotlessly clean. If it isn't, the owner clearly doesn't care about the club or its members. The equipment must be properly maintained with basic care such as regular inspection and tightening of all dumbbells, barbells, and machines. It's incredibly frustrating when you're training and some guide rod on a machine sticks because someone failed to lubricate the machine properly. There's no excuse for this. A good gym will clean the guide rods and re-silicone them at least two times per week.

The locker room and shower facility should be immaculate. Think of the gym as if it were your home—if you don't get that same good, comfortable feeling in the gym that you do at your home, it's time for you to start looking for another gym.

With so many health clubs to choose from, you're in the driver's seat when it comes to finding the best gym at the best price. Never forget that. Of course, getting the greatest value for your gym membership dollar is important, but don't let that be the sole criterion for your decision. Using these recommendations, along with your own requirements, you'll find the right gym for you.

DO UNTO OTHERS: RULES OF THE GYM

Okay, so you've picked a gym, and now it's time to get in there and get incredibly huge, strong, ripped, and in-shape. Whoa, Nelly—before you go blastin', you need to learn some etiquette. I'm talking gym etiquette. Many practice it; others don't. Think about it: there are more pleasant things to do than wait for a piece of equipment and then have to wipe the sweat off it!

Many of today's bodybuilders and fitness athletes don't pay much attention to gym etiquette. It's time they did. Let me suggest some easy-to-follow rules that will add to the quality of your workout experience. Although these rules sound simple, you wouldn't believe how many people ignore or are unaware of them. Take heed: in many clubs, violating these simple rules can cost you your membership!

Rule 1

Put the Weights Back After You've Used Them

How often have you wasted valuable time searching for a pair of dumbbells, only to find them in two different places? That aggravating delay breaks the rhythm of your workout and causes you to lose concentration, focus, and intensity. Always put the weights back in their proper place when you are through with them.

Rule 2

Never Walk in Front of or Otherwise Distract Someone Doing an Exercise

Picture this: you're seated on an upright bench doing dumbbell presses. Your eyes are focused like laser beams on your delts in the mirror. Then, nonchalantly, some joker steps in front of you to get a weight. And how about the guy or gal who wants to chat when you're in the middle of an all-out set? Talk about a no-brainer. Stifle your automatic reaction to these rude acts. Politely tell them how you feel. Also practice what you preach and set a good example for them.

Rule 3

Always Wipe Your Equipment After Use

Wiping another person's sweat off a bench or machine is about as much fun as a swift kick in the shin. Show some courtesy and always try to leave the equipment in better condition than you found it.

Rule 4

Don't Drop, Throw Down, or Bang the Weights

I must admit, guys are the biggest violators of this rule. I don't know how many times I've seen a dude finish lifting heavy tonnage and then drop the weight on the floor. Not only is this distracting, but it damages the equipment.

Many times after repeated abuse, dumbbells must be tightened. The professional clubs and gyms won't tolerate this kind of equipment abuse, and neither should you. When it happens, tell the club management about it. Remember: you're in the gym to work out, not to be the gym mechanic.

Rule 5

Don't Spit in the Drinking Fountain

Boy, there's nothing more inviting than going to the drinking fountain for a cool, refreshing drink and seeing a big phlegmmer or wad of gum lying there. Wow, the person who does this in the drinking fountain has a lot of class; too bad it's all third. Show a sense of decency, hygiene, and elegance, and don't be a Mr. or Ms. Drain Clog.

Rule 6

Unload the Plates from the Machines After Your Exercise

Granted, for most people, having a couple of 45-pound plates left on the leg press, hack squat, or bench press machine is no problem. Where things get a bit insane is when someone finishes a 1,200-pound leg press and leaves all the plates for the next person to unload. Definitely not a good time. Show consideration for others and unload your weights after you've finished blastin' your body.

Rule 7

Follow the Golden Rule

Always talk about how great this *Bodybuilding 101* book is. Okay, seriously, this rule says it all: Have respect for others in the gym, and treat them the way you'd like to be treated.

Let's face it, just because you may be bigger, stronger, prettier, wealthier, or whatever than others, you shouldn't expect preferential treatment in the gym. We're all of equal importance. Think about your actions in the gym. If more of us would think about others, we'd greatly increase the enjoyment and results from our workouts.

> **"The greatest thing about man is his ability to transcend himself, his ancestry, and his environment and to become what he dreams of being."**
>
> **–Tully C. Knoles**

Don't you ever let your friends, family, or anyone else tell you that you cannot build the body you dream of or have the life you want, because you can! The majority of people are like sheep, living their lives for the approval of others and following the crowd and its beliefs. You were given the incredible body you have and the dreams in your heart because you can achieve anything you deeply desire. The others have no idea what that's like, because they've listened to the voice of fear that has lied to them their whole lives. You're different, and because of how incredible you are, you have a life waiting for you to experience what all those other people will only dream of. Always listen to your heart and follow where it leads you.

6

Do You Need a Training Partner?

The Pros and Cons of Forming an Ironclad Partnership

The business of building the body is the goal. To do it right requires a good plan. To make that plan successful more quickly, many bodybuilders enlist a training partner. Some bodybuilders swear by them; others would rather not be bothered. Before you decide whether it would be beneficial to train with a partner, consider the following pros and cons.

THE PROS

Spotting and Pushing

An obvious benefit of having a training partner is the ability to handle more weight in your workouts. One of the primary functions of a partner is to push you through those last few reps that you couldn't or wouldn't normally conquer on your own. This greatly increases the intensity of your workouts. Also, an extra measure of safety is present when your partner is spotting you. If you have trouble handling the weight, your partner can help you "cheat" through the rep or simply grab the bar and put it back in its proper place.

Creating New Routines

A training partner can help you experiment and open your eyes to new routines. For example, let's say you and your partner have been using a certain routine for awhile. The next time you work out, you suggest combining your two favorite body part exercises with your partner's two favorites. Or maybe during the workout, your partner suggests an exercise or a combination of exercises that gives both of you great results. Many bodybuilders sometimes pick someone in the gym to work out with and then follow the other person's routine, just to do something different and keep it fresh so the body will stay off-guard and growing.

Observing

Using proper form is crucial to making the muscle work through the maximum contraction. Many times it takes only a slight variation in form to turn a good exercise into a great one. Your partner can keenly observe your form, give you feedback on how to correct it, and instruct you on the proper way to do it. All the greats, from the legendary

John Grimek and Steve Reeves to today's champions, say that good form is *vital* to making muscles work and grow! A good training partner can help you achieve that.

Motivation

Let's face it—some days you may not feel like training. Maybe you didn't get enough sleep, your job is causing you stress, or you didn't eat enough. Whatever the reason, you just don't feel like hitting the weights. But when you have a training partner who's depending on you to work out, somehow you manage to get in the gym. Many of the top pros say they've had their best workouts on days they didn't want to train, but showed up anyway because they knew their training partner was in the gym waiting.

THE CONS

Hey, Where Are You?

On the flip side, sometimes a partner may not show up at the gym. Bummer—when the quality of your workout depends on his help. If this happens more than once, get a new partner.

Compromise Is the Key

Sometimes a training partner will get locked into a fixed way of training and will be unwilling to compromise. Trying new exercises, using new angles, and varying weight and rep schemes can add variety and excitement to the workout. How are you going to find the best training program for you and your partner unless you compromise and experiment? The best pro bodybuilders

constantly search for new and varied ways to stimulate strength and growth. So should you. If your partner won't budge, you both suffer.

What the Heck Are Our Training Goals?

If you're training for cuts and your partner is training for power, do you think there might be a conflict? You bet there is. That's why both of you should discuss routines, exercises, sets, reps, weight, days on and off, and other variables that will help you reach your training goals. When you and your partner agree on specific goals, compromising on your training routine will be no problem.

Hey—Slow Down!

Even if your partner is dependable and you both share the same training goals, you may still encounter a problem: recovery time. You may be quite different from your partner in how quickly you recover from a set or a workout. Let's say that you're able to recover much more quickly. There's a good chance that you may eventually feel that your partner's holding you back. Here's where you have to weigh the pros and cons of having a training partner. Maybe you'd be better off without one—or maybe you just need a different partner. Only you can accurately judge whether the benefits you receive from having a training partner outweigh the detriment.

A competent, compatible training partner can add immeasurably to the intensity of your workouts and help you achieve your bodybuilding goals more quickly. But whether you choose to train with a partner or alone, one imperative remains: enjoy your workouts!

7

Gymspeak: You Gotta Know the Lingo

Bodybuilding Definitions (of words, that is)

So you walk into the gym for your first workout and you see this gorgeous woman. "Hey," you say, "you're looking good!" "Thanks," she replies. "It's been the negatives."

Huh? What are the negatives? Is that like when you give people a hard time with your bad attitude?

Yes, bodybuilding has its own lingo. Every sport does. It can get confusing. To help eliminate such confusion, here's some gymspeak to help you become bodybuilder fluent.

Collar—No, this is not something that goes around your neck or the dog's. It slips on the ends of the barbell or dumbbell and is tightened snugly against the weights so they won't slip off during exercise. Be sure to use them.

Deadlift—Wrong, it's not an action a pallbearer performs at a funeral. A deadlift is a powerlifting movement usually performed on a power platform that is used to build the lower back, legs, and trapezius.

Dips—You won't find these at a party. Dips are performed on an apparatus resembling two parallel bars three to four feet high. This exercise is great for the chest and triceps.

Dumbbell—This isn't someone who acts goofy. Dumbbells are those small weights you can hold in each hand. They may be small, but they can be heavy—some are over 200 pounds each!

Ez-curl bar—No, not some new hair-care product. The EZ-curl bar is a curved bar used primarily for biceps and triceps work. Also commonly called an *EZ-bar*.

Fast-twitch fibers—This isn't a new breakfast cereal that causes your body to do crazy things. It simply refers to muscle cells that fire quickly and are used primarily in anaerobic activities like sprinting and powerlifting.

Flyes—These aren't those annoying little creatures that buzz in your ear. Flyes are a chest exercise performed with dumbbells on a flat, decline, or incline bench.

Freeweights—No, you don't take these home without paying for them. *Freeweights* refer to all those round weight plates you see on barbells, dumbbells, and weight racks.

French press—This is not journalism in France. It's an exercise used to build the triceps, and can be performed either standing, seated, or lying down on a bench using a straight bar, curved bar, rope, dumbbells, or machine.

Isokinetic—*Isokinetic* describes a type of exercise in which there is accommodating resistance. Machines are supposed to vary the amount of resistance being lifted to match the power output of the muscle.

Isometric—*Isometric* exercise involves muscular contraction in which the muscle maintains a constant length and joints do not move. The exercises are usually performed against a wall or other immovable object.

Isotonic—*Isotonic* exercise involves muscular action in which there is a change in length of muscle and weight, keeping tension constant. Working with freeweights is a classic isotonic exercise.

Negatives—These have nothing to do with a bad attitude. *Negatives* refer to a technique of resisting the weight while lowering it against gravity.

Peaking—This can refer to two things: Any exercise situation in which you can get maximal isolation of a specific muscle being worked. Or, bodybuilders who are getting ready for a competition

or just want to have the maximum degree of muscular definition and the least body fat.

Power rack—Nice try, but this is not a swift kick in the groin. It's a safety apparatus that has two thick, adjustable steel pins that the barbell rests upon. Bodybuilders and powerlifters use the power rack to perform squats, shrugs, deadlifts, and presses.

Progressive Resistance—As the name implies, this is simply increasing the weight as muscles gain strength and endurance.

Pump—Not a lady's shoe or tire accessory. A pump is the ecstatic feeling you get while performing an exercise as the muscle being worked swells with blood. Many bodybuilders consider this a prime indicator of whether an exercise is working.

Slow-twitch fibers—These are composed of those muscle cells that contract slowly, are resistant to fatigue, and are used in endurance activities like long-distance running, cycling, and swimming.

Striations—Many times after a bodybuilder has achieved maximum muscularity and minimum body fat, *striations* occur. Striations are the linear details across a muscle that look like fine lines.

Vascularity—Whenever you see a bodybuilder with veins that stand out, that's vascularity. This condition, which combines maximum muscle with minimum fat, can be achieved through diet, weight, and cardiovascular training.

The next time you go to the gym, listen closely to what people are saying. Chances are, having learned these definitions, you'll know what they're talking about.

"All rising to a great place is by a winding stair."

—Francis Bacon

The road you'll take to reaching your fitness and bodybuilding dreams is never straight. Like all things in life, the many roads we take to follow our dreams are winding, crooked, at times rough, other times smooth, but never the same. And all along those roads are rest stops—places where you are to stop and learn the lessons that life wants to teach you at that special time in your life—before you're allowed to travel on that road again. Learn the lesson, and you're well on your way. However, keep thinking that you'll continue to do things your way and not learn the lesson, and you'll be on the road again alright—but that different road will take you right back to that same rest stop over and over until you learn the lesson. Learn the lesson, and you'll enjoy the drive that will take you to whatever great place you want to go.

8

Personal Trainers

Do You Need One?

One of the biggest changes in the fitness scene during recent years is the proliferation of personal trainers. Go to any gym and you'll see what I mean! Many people have asked me questions about personal trainers: *Do I need one? What should I look for in a personal trainer? What kind of qualifications should they have?* The list goes on. Let's take a closer look at personal trainers.

A GOLD MINE OF INFORMATION

Simply stated, a personal trainer's job is to get you in shape. You're paying good money for him or her to be your coach, teach you the mechanics of exercising, show you the various exercises you can do to achieve your fitness goals based on your body type, motivate and inspire you, and teach you proper exercise form in order to avoid injury.

A good personal trainer can be a gold mine. She can save you years of frustration and hours of wasted effort simply by correcting improper technique and bad eating habits. One of my training philosophies is to take all the

time I need to learn how to train properly, and build that foundation. With that knowledge, you can experience years of enjoyable workouts and expect great results. If your personal trainer can help you build that foundation, he will be worth every penny you spend for his services.

A good personal trainer doesn't necessarily become useless after you become an advanced bodybuilder. Quite a few of the pros in California have personal trainers.

THE COST OF BAD ADVICE

From the letters I've received, many people have been deceived by so-called personal trainers. Many well-intentioned individuals become personal trainers because they want to help people, work in the fitness industry, do enjoyable work, and get a good paycheck. Many of these people, with little or no academic training, claim to be experts in kinesiology, physiology, biomechanics, and nutrition. However, very few actually are.

But personal trainers have a primary obligation to their clients. Their clients' health and welfare rest squarely on their shoulders. And many people have had their health put at risk by bad advice from unqualified personal trainers. Improper exercise form, using too much weight or undertaking an advanced routine too soon can lead to problems.

The same goes for nutritional advice and supplementation. Those not properly trained to give such advice are not only committing a disservice to their clients, they are risking their well-being, too.

TAKE A MILLIONAIRE'S SUGGESTION

When people come to the gym or begin working out, they're very impressionable. They want results, and they don't have all the information it takes to achieve them. They devour training information found in books and magazines, talk to friends and other people in the gym, and some turn to personal trainers.

But often the novice looking for a personal trainer has no way of knowing who is qualified, especially when many of them look good and sound like they know what they're talking about.

Please understand something: I'm not against personal trainers. Many of them are good friends of mine, and I know that they help great numbers of people. The problem I have—as with any profession—is that many personal trainers are unqualified. They pass themselves off as experts, when in truth they have no expertise at all.

I once heard a very wealthy man give some young guy a great piece of advice. The millionaire said, "If you want to learn how to be wealthy, ask someone who has a lot of money." The same advice goes for personal trainers.

If you want to be in great shape, look for someone who is in great shape *and* is certified by a respected accrediting organization.

SEPARATING THE WHEAT FROM THE CHAFF: THE TOP CERTIFICATION PROGRAMS

Asking someone whether he is a certified personal trainer can get confusing. Many will correctly respond yes; more than 2,000 personal trainer certification programs are offered in the United States!

As of this writing, very few states have any regulations regarding personal trainers. This could change in the near future. Until then, you need to pick a personal trainer who has passed some tough qualification requirements from a well-respected organization.

I could recommend many personal trainer certification programs. However, space doesn't permit me to list all of them. Here are a few good ones:

- The National Strength and Conditioning Association: (719) 632-6722
- The American College of Sports Medicine: (317) 637-9200
- The National Academy of Sports Medicine: (312) 929-5101
- The International Sports Sciences Association: (800) 892-4772
- The American Council on Exercise: (800) 529-8227

THE BOTTOM LINE

Ultimately, you must decide whether having a personal trainer will be beneficial to you. You can listen to your friends who have personal trainers, but I suggest standing back for a moment and taking a good look at the results. In this case, results do speak much louder than words.

9

Don't Be Fooled

Cutting Through the Hype

I'm going to give it to you straight. Bodybuilders are being taken advantage of through misleading ads, products, and gimmicks. I wish it weren't true, but it is. Let's try to make some sense of this stuff.

When I was a beginning bodybuilder, my life was focused on training. I read the muscle magazines religiously. I talked with many knowledgeable people about training, diet, and supplementation. I believed much of what I read and heard—and then gradually my eyes opened.

Many of those sacred beliefs were shaken when I learned what really happens in a small part of the bodybuilding world. Many of those products and claims that sound too good to be true *are* too good to be true.

How do I know? In my travels all over the world, I've talked in depth to pro bodybuilders and people just like you and me who love to train and want great results through natural means. And I've observed, not only in bodybuilding but in everyday life as well, that the most successful people question everything they see and hear. They

put that information to the test to find out whether it's true. That's exactly what you should do. Get all the facts—at least as much information as you can—then make a judicious decision.

I asked many of the world's top bodybuilders what they think about these new products, ads, and gimmicks. Based on their comments, here are the best of bodybuilding's do and don't beliefs.

THE PROS DO BELIEVE THAT . . .

- Hard training, a well-balanced diet, and rest are the most important factors in their bodybuilding success.
- Vitamins and minerals are important—most pros take them.
- Amino acids (peptide bond and branched-chain) can help speed recovery.
- Supplemental creatine works well for some people and not so well for others.
- Protein powders (whey, egg, or milk and egg) can help support

gains in lean muscle mass and weight.

- Carbohydrate drinks (about 50 grams taken within 30 minutes after a workout) are very effective at helping the body replenish muscle glycogen.

THE PROS DON'T BELIEVE THAT . . .

- You can radically change a body in 90 days.
- A secret supplement from a foreign country is the cure-all/end-all for muscle growth and strength.
- There is only one way to train or that one training system is best.
- One supplement is responsible for a bodybuilder's success, or that you can reach your full bodybuilding potential *unless* you take a balanced approach to weight training (routines, exercises, diet, supplementation, rest).

WHAT AM I SAYING?

Ours is a great sport, and the benefits of weight training go far beyond just improving appearance. The majority of people in the bodybuilding industry are there because they love the sport and want to see people like you succeed and reach your bodybuilding goals. That's why they provide the products and services they do—to help you.

My advice comes from the heart. I can relate to who and what you are and where you come from, and I'm thankful for having the privilege of living in the bodybuilding and fitness world that you read about. Along with that privilege comes a sense of duty to tell it to you straight, based upon my own experience and the experiences of many of the world's best pros.

Ah, but don't just take my advice. Remember, be a seeker of truth and put to the test those things that you see, read, and hear. But that doesn't mean you should spend all of your hard-earned money doing so. Ask questions. Write to the manufacturers and providers of these services and get information. The reputable ones will be glad to provide you with the facts you seek. Those who have the best reputations and have lasted in this business have done so by not misleading people. In bodybuilding, as in any other science, only truth can stand the test of time.

"Did you ever hear of a man who had striven all his life faithfully and singly toward an object, and in no measure obtained it? If a man constantly aspires, is he not elevated?"

—Henry David Thoreau

Looking and feeling great is important to you, right? You bet it is, and I applaud you for all the hard work, discipline, belief, and desire you have. And didn't it seem at times, even when you were making little or no progress and felt like you were just going through the motions, that something inside you was growing? That's the way life is. The outside appearance can be very deceptive, because it rarely shows immediately all the incredible changes that are taking place on the inside every single day. Keep the faith and belief, no matter what the outside might look like, because it's guaranteed that you're growing in more ways than you know and see.

10

Your Training Textbook

When You Finish This Course, Your Diploma Is Awarded with Muscle

Congratulations! By making a commitment to the bodybuilding lifestyle, you've taken the first step to looking and feeling great. But, as with all endeavors, you must understand the principles and instructions in order to reap the greatest benefits. With its own set of parameters and guidelines, bodybuilding can offer you a lifetime of looking and feeling great, providing you understand the basics.

Enough talk. Let's get right into it with this chapter's topic: training for the beginner. You have to get used to a few things when you start training: the first is muscle soreness. Soreness is simply the body's response to muscles having been worked in a new and different way.

For the beginner, slight soreness is normal and can last a few days. If you've pushed your muscles too hard, severe soreness can result. As a general rule, if your body is still sore on the day you are scheduled to work out, give yourself an extra day of rest for additional recuperation. In time, your body will adapt and recover more quickly as you continue to train.

Another change you'll experience: the way your body looks. When you start out, you may see your body literally changing by the week! This is one of the most phenomenal results of the initial exposure to regular bodybuilding training.

SAMPLE BEGINNING PROGRAM

We've been talking about beginner training. Now here's a quick review that will get you going and growing faster than ever.

Schedule

Monday—2 sets of 10 reps per body part

Tuesday—rest

Wednesday—2 sets of 10 reps per body part

Thursday—rest

Friday—2 sets of 10 reps per body part

Saturday—rest

Sunday—rest

Exercises

Pick one from each category every workout.

Chest—Barbell flat bench press, barbell incline press

Back—Chin-up, pulldown, row, deadlift

Shoulders—Press, lateral raise, upright row

Triceps—Pressdown, French press, kickback

Biceps—Barbell curl, seated dumbbell curl

Thighs—Squat, leg extension, leg curl

Calves—Calf raise (standing, seated, or donkey)

Abs—Crunch

TRAINING FREQUENCY

How often you train is as important as how you train.

Balancing Work and Recuperation

Training the whole body three days a week (Monday, Wednesday, and Friday, for example) is ideal for the beginner. This allows you nearly 48 hours of rest between workouts and gives you an additional two days of rest over the weekend. I suggest doing one or two exercises of 2 sets of 10 reps per body part.

You may feel like doing more, but don't. Give yourself at least a month of this type of training before doing more exercises. This will allow your body the proper stimulation for growth without overtaxing its ability to recuperate.

As you progress, you may decide to do more advanced training, such as working specific body parts in some workouts, with whole-body sessions only two times a week. Examples of such training include the double-split, the push–pull system, four-on/one-off, and three-on/one-off.

Your decision to get into new types of training depends on how rapidly your body adapts to each new level of training, and your individual goals. You may be ready to go beyond the three-days-a-week workout after only one month of training. Someone else may decide that three days per week is ideal for her lifestyle and goals. *Stay on the beginner program for at least four months.*

Sets and reps are important factors in your bodybuilding success. *A good set is made up of good reps, and a good workout is made up of both.* At this point in your training, doing more than 2 sets of 10 reps per body part greatly increases your chances of overtraining (doing too much work and getting inadequate rest, leading to diminished gains). Ten reps provides optimal muscle stimulation without putting your body into a state of over- or undertraining.

Here, too, as your body improves in strength and condition, you may decide to use supersets; giant sets; pyramid training; staggered sets; high-, moderate-, or low-rep training; rest–pause; volume training; speed training; and many other advanced techniques, as a way of increasing the intensity of your workouts for maximum growth. (I'll discuss these variations soon.)

Beginners often ask, *How do I know when to increase the weight on the exercises I do?* Once you're able to do 10 reps fairly easily with a given weight, try increasing the weight by 10 percent. Let's say you can bench press 135 pounds for 10 easy reps. On your next set, try going up to 145 to 150 pounds for 10 reps. Do this on all your exercises. This is the heart of progressive resistance training, which is the best way to gain size and strength.

**Avoiding the Big Mistake:
Why More Is Not Better**

Far too many beginning bodybuilders fall victim to the "If some is good, more is better" mentality. That makes no sense! Your body needs time to adjust to the exercise you're asking it to do.

One exercise per body part may not sound like enough to produce any results—but if you're a beginner, it will. As you continue to train and your body adapts to the exercise and recuperative demands you place upon it, you'll be able to add more sets and exercises to your routine.

Be patient and don't overtrain. Overtraining will halt your progress and increase your chances of injury. It takes time to build a great body, but the rewards are worth it!

GO WITH THE BASICS

Starting out with the basic exercises is something that you'll be grateful for later on down the road. The basic exercises let your body get used to the proper groove for each movement. You've got to know how to do an exercise correctly before you can get the maximum benefit from it.

The basic exercises should form the foundation of your bodybuilding program both now and in the future. Stay away from cables and machines at this point—they'll be important to your training later on. Concentrate on mastering the basic movements. Almost all bodybuilding champions in the sport today still use basic movements as the cornerstone of their training routines.

One of the most important elements in laying the proper foundation for your fitness success is using good form on every exercise. Using good form means doing every exercise and every rep with complete control through the full range of motion. *Incomplete reps build incomplete body parts*, so always keep the weight under strict control throughout the full range of motion. Don't be so concerned with how much you can lift. Concentrate on feeling the exercise and working the muscle completely. I can't stress this enough.

Without a doubt, sloppy form is a major cause of injury to muscles and connective tissue. Don't forget that an injury can sideline you for days, weeks, or even months! Your time is valuable. When you go to the gym, you want results, not injuries and little or no progress. Use good form on every exercise, and you'll avoid the injuries while getting the results you seek.

PART II

You're No Longer a Beginner

11

Intermediate Bodybuilding

Goals, Expectations, Weights, Proper Form,
Training Logs, Nutrition

Have you been on a beginner's body-building program for at least four months? If so, consider yourself a candidate for an intermediate program. After a minimum of four solid months, your beginner's program should have given you a good working knowledge of the basic exercises.

It also should have allowed you

- to find your best exercise grooves;
- sufficient time to gain muscle and connective tissue strength;
- to gradually use heavier weights; and
- to observe which body parts have grown the fastest and become the strongest.

OBSERVATIONS FROM THE CHAMPS: WHY THEY DO WHAT THEY DO

Genetics aside, champion bodybuilders are not much different than you and me. The difference, if one exists, lies in the fact that they have found the best ways of putting exercises, angles, weights, reps, and sets together in their workouts to give them consistently good results.

Many of these pros—especially the older champions of years past—train in very unconventional ways. How about training biceps every day for seven days just to shock the stubborn body part into growth? What about doing 10 sets of 10-rep squats, three times a week for two weeks, to pack on leg mass? Hey,

don't laugh. These guys got great results doing those things.

So what's the lesson here? Don't get locked into one way of training just because you read about it or someone told you to do it. You're the only one who has your genetic structure, goals, and particular desire.

You must train your body according to those factors, and that means developing your own specialized routines. Experiment, experiment, experiment! Never let your body become stale by using the same old routine time and time again. Be different. Go ahead and be selfish here and start growing!

So what would you like to do? Gain more muscle mass? Lose a few pounds? Tighten up? Whatever you want, you can have it.

IT'S ALL ABOUT INTENSITY

Just remember, it's not how long you train that matters; it's what you do when you train. For example, your best buddy might work out for two hours, but with above-average intensity. Yet if you work out for only 30 minutes but do it with 100-percent, all-out intensity, you'll get far better results! Intensity makes the difference.

For our purposes, think of intensity as how hard and effectively you can make a muscle work during a given period. Obviously, if your chest workout calls for 12 sets and you've just finished your second, do you really think you'll be able to train with all-out intensity for the next 10 sets? Don't kid yourself.

However, if you've just done your second set for chest and you've only got three more sets to do, you'll probably be able to give those remaining sets all you've got. *When the number of sets becomes your primary workout goal, you miss the whole point of bodybuilding, which is working a muscle with maximum intensity for maximum results.*

THE ABC'S OF INTERMEDIATE TRAINING

With the beginner program, you trained the whole body three times per week. Now it's time to get into split training, where you'll work out four days per week, but train the entire body only twice.

The four-day split is one of the best training programs around. You'll work upper body one day, legs the next, rest a day, hit upper body again, then legs again on the fifth day; and then you'll take two days off from training.

The four-day split allows you to do more exercises, handle more weight, and train each body part more intensely; it also gives your body adequate time for recuperation, which translates into growth and strength.

What Can You Expect from This New Program?

First of all, you can expect to gain some serious size and strength. You're going to do more exercises and sets, handle more weight, and execute a bit of specialization work for those weak body parts.

Your body will start to become a high-performance machine. It will handle much more intensive work, and in the process it will adapt to those demands wonderfully. You will get more out of your body than ever before. Not only that, you're also going to blast through self-imposed preconceptions about just how good your body can look and feel.

The Exercises

As you recall, your beginner program emphasized the use of basic exercises performed with barbells and dumbbells. Your intermediate program will keep those core exercises, but add cables and machines. For any muscle to grow, you must work it hard and from a variety of angles—and that means using whatever modality of training is at your disposal.

THE INTERMEDIATE PROGRAM—FOUR-DAY SPLIT

Monday and Thursday—Upper Body

Exercise	Sets	Reps
Chest		
Barbell incline press	3	6–8
Dumbbell press	3	8–10
Flat bench flye	2	10–12
Back		
Chin-up *or*	3	limit
machine pulldown	3	12–15
Dumbbell row	2	8
Seated cable row	2	8–10
Deadlift (only once per week)	3	6
Shoulders		
Seated dumbbell press	3	8–10
Dumbbell side lateral	3	10–14
Barbell shrug	2	5–8
Biceps		
Seated dumbbell incline curl	3	6–9
Ez-bar preacher curl	3	10–15
Triceps		
Pressdown	4	12–18
Lying Ez-bar extension	3	8–10
Abs		
Hanging knee raise	3	limit
Crunch	3	8–10

Flat bench flye (a)   **Flat bench flye (b)**

Dumbbell row (a)   **Dumbbell row (b)**   **Dumbbell side lateral**

Seated dumbbell incline curl (a)   **Seated dumbbell incline curl (b)**

Lying Ez-bar extension (a)   **Lying Ez-bar extension (b)**

Hanging knee raise (a)   **Hanging knee raise (b)**   *continued on next page*

THE INTERMEDIATE PROGRAM—FOUR-DAY SPLIT *(continued)*

Tuesday and Friday—Lower Body

Exercise	Sets	Reps
Legs		
Leg extension (for warm-up)	2	15–20
Front squat	4	8–10
Leg press (feet wide, toes		
pointed out)	3	10–20
Leg curl	4	12–20
Standing leg curl	3	10–15
Standing calf raise	4	8–20
Seated calf raise	3	8–12
Wednesday, Saturday, and Sunday—Rest		

Leg press (a)

Leg press (b)

Seated calf raise (a)

Seated calf raise (b)

PROPER FORM

Continually strive to lift heavier weight whenever possible, but keep in mind that to make a muscle grow you must work it with intensity. Proper form is an important prerequisite for muscle growth. You can use terrible form and still intensely work and overload a muscle; however, you do so at great risk of injury. Feel every rep. If the weight you're using doesn't allow that, by all means reduce it. *The majority of bodybuilders would do well to remember that weight is only a means to an end and never an end itself.*

THE WEIGHTS

At this point, you should have a good idea regarding the amount of weight you can handle for the basic movements. While I strongly believe that you should warm up thoroughly before

heavy lifting, I also believe that you shouldn't waste valuable time and energy once you're warmed up.

For example, let's say you're doing dumbbell presses, and your best is using 60-pound dumbbells for 6 to 8

reps. On your first two warm-up sets, do 30 pounds for 10 reps. Then on your first heavy set, go right to the 60s and crank out 6 to 8 or more reps. On your second heavy set, reduce the weight by 10 percent and crank out another 6 to 8 reps. Third set, reduce the weight by another 10 percent and bang out another 6 to 8 reps. You're then finished with that movement.

YOUR CHANGING NUTRITION NEEDS

Your intermediate diet should remain very similar to the beginner diet outlined earlier in the book: high complex carbs, moderate protein, and low fat. However, because you're adding an extra day of training and increasing workout intensity, we'll raise the carbs and protein a bit. You may want to start supplementing with branched-chain amino acids (BCAAS) before and after your workouts.

First of all, to restore depleted muscle glycogen, always have a carb drink (at least 50 grams, and some bodybuilders will have as much as 150 grams) within 30 minutes after your workout. This 30-minute time period after the workout is extremely important for refueling muscle and liver glycogen.

About 40 minutes after you have the carb drink, have a good protein meal. If that's not possible, then be sure to have a good meal of carbs and protein within 90 minutes after your workout. Of course, keep your water intake high throughout the day—at least 80 ounces, and more if possible.

I'll tell you a trick that has helped me keep my waist size down while I gained muscle mass. On the meal immediately following my workout and on the days my body was sore, I doubled my protein intake—sometimes tripled it! After the soreness reached its peak and began to diminish, I slowly lowered my protein intake until it was back down to normal maintenance levels. My carb and fat intake remained consistent. Doing this helped give my body the extra protein it needed when it needed it. And my body recovered much more quickly from the hard workouts. Try it and watch what happens.

KEEP STRESS LEVELS LOW

The four-day split program will tax your recuperative capacities more than the three-day beginner program. That's why I suggest that you get in the gym, work out very intensely, and get the heck out!

Another thing I strongly advise is not to train too late at night. Training too close to bedtime can keep you awake and prevent you from getting the recommended seven to nine hours of sleep each night.

And a word about getting frustrated with your workouts . . . don't! Seriously, if today's workout didn't allow you to lift any heavier, do more reps, or get a better pump, no big deal. In the grand scheme of things, as it relates to your body and fitness, it won't make any difference. Be kind to yourself and tell yourself that with the next workout you'll do better. End of story. Now rest and enjoy!

WHEN TO CHANGE YOUR WORKOUTS

By all means, constantly vary your workouts. With each workout, use different exercise combinations, reps, weights, angles, and rest periods. Any or all of the warning signs that follow might indicate that it's time to change your workouts:

- No increases in weights used
- Little, if any, muscle or strength gains
- Boredom
- You've been on the same program for six weeks or more

This intermediate routine is meant solely as a guide. Use it and keep only those exercises that work for you; throw away the rest. Experiment and find other exercises that give you great results, and use them regularly.

However, always change the order and other workout variables to keep your body off guard. The bottom line is to keep your workouts fresh and exciting. Is that really possible? Of course!

WHEN TO MOVE TO THE NEXT LEVEL

Stay on the intermediate program for at least five months. Remember, this four-day split is so good that many of the top pros—who have been training for years—still use it! Forget the goofy standing-on-a-bench-and-pulling-a-cable-through-your-legs-for-a-deadlift–type exercises. Stay with the basic barbell and dumbbell exercises, along with selected machines.

The kind of exercises you do isn't as important as you may think. Sure, certain exercises are necessary to work certain muscles. However, *how effectively you make that exercise work a particular body part is what determines the results.* The sooner you give up on looking for a magical exercise to change a body part, the sooner you'll start using your own mind and finding your own creative ways to make any exercise work for you!

INTENSITY PRINCIPLES

I've talked a lot about intensity. Are you catching the drift as to just how important it is to your bodybuilding success? Good. I'm going to continue our intensity discussion by giving you some excellent intermediate-level intensity principles that will kick your body into some serious growth.

- **Superset**—In this technique, you group two exercises together for opposing muscle groups—for example, biceps curls and triceps pressdowns. As soon as you finish the set of biceps curls, immediately do a set of triceps pressdowns.

- **Pyramid**—This technique requires increasing the weight you use each set. For example, begin your first set with 60 percent of your one-rep max weight, and increase the weight by 10 percent each succeeding set. You can also do the opposite: warm up for a few sets, use your heaviest weight for 6 to 8 reps, then decrease the weight by 10 percent each succeeding set.
- **Compound set**—This technique involves performing two back-to-back exercises for the same body part—with little or no rest—for example, doing barbell curls immediately followed by a set of seated dumbbell incline curls.
- **Cycle training**—Cycle training is simply changing how you work your body on a regular basis. For a few weeks, you may want to lift heavier weights and do fewer reps. Other times, you might want to use lighter weights and do more

reps. Many bodybuilders who train heavy all the time are at greater risk of injury than those who cycle their training. Three cycles you should be concerned with are as follows:
- **Mass cycle**—Moderate to heavy weights; no more than 90 seconds of rest between sets; 6 to 10 reps for upper body and 8 to 20 reps for lower body.
- **Power cycle**—Heavy weights; 3 to 8 reps for lower- and upper-body movements; up to three minutes of rest between sets.
- **Cut cycle**—Light to moderate weights; 12 to 25 reps; no more than 45 seconds of rest between sets.

  Stay on each cycle for six to eight weeks, and take one full week off from training before moving to the next cycle.
- **Isotension**—Feeling a muscle work is the key to getting the most from any exercise. To help create this mind–muscle link, regularly practice isotension. This is a technique in which—without using any weights—you flex the muscle you've been working and hold it in the peak contracted position for three to six seconds. Do this three times at the end of the last set of every body part workout.
- **Muscle confusion**—Your body adapts very quickly to the physical demands you place upon it. If you do the same routine in the same way over and over, your body will stop responding. That's why you must change your workouts, exercises, sets, reps, weights, rest periods, angles, and degrees of intensity every time you work out. By doing so, you will keep your body off-guard and you'll continue to grow and get stronger.

THE IMPORTANCE OF A TRAINING LOG

A training log is the basis for forming excellent future routines. You'll soon have completed so many workouts that those record-setting lifts and great routine combinations will be only fuzzy memories unless you write them down.

Making your own personal training log is an excellent way to deduce which combinations of exercises, sets, reps, weight, rest periods, angles, and intensity work best for your body. It's easy to do. During or at the end of each workout, write down the following:

- Body parts trained
- Exercises and the order in which they were performed
- Weight used and the number of reps done for each set
- General comments after the workout—for example, *I did 10 reps with 225 pounds on the squat* or *I went five pounds heavier with 4 extra reps on the bench press*
- Postworkout comments such as *My upper chest was really sore for three days!* or *The triceps routine really gave me a good pump but I didn't get sore*

"It's never too late to start again . . . and it's always too early to quit."

You can have the body you want and look and feel great no matter what your age. Of course, a 50-year-old man or woman may have a tough time getting the body of a 20-year-old—but the 50-year-olds I know couldn't care less. You see, the biggest thing that holds people back from whatever they want in life is themselves. They'll tell you it's other people, or their job, or their family, or spouse, or whatever else; but when you peel off the layers of excuses, all that remains is themselves. You might as well throw all those familiar excuses out the door right now, because I'm not accepting them and neither should you. Whatever it is you want, do it now and you'll enjoy it for the rest of your life.

12

The Dirty Dozen:
Common Training Mistakes

I keep going to the gym, but feel like I'm just going through the motions. Why can't I get better results? Ah, yes, the body-builder blues—rather, the overtraining blues. Without a doubt, overtraining is the biggest cause of poor bodybuilding and lack of strength progress around. Try as you may, inevitably at some point in your training you'll probably ask yourself how you can get better results.

Maybe you need to change your routine. Possibly an extra day of rest is all that's needed. Are you eating a proper bodybuilding diet with good supplementation? The list goes on. One thing's for sure: you need to look at your total training plan to know what needs to be changed. Knowing what training mistakes to avoid can be a huge step forward. Here are some of the most common:

Overtraining

If your workouts take longer than 90 minutes, you're overtraining. Many of the world's best bodybuilders' workouts take less than 45 minutes! It's not how much time you spend in the gym, but what you accomplish while you're there that matters.

Poor Form and Incomplete Movements

Not only does poor form cause injuries, it doesn't allow for complete muscle-fiber stimulation. The key to making a muscle grow is to make the muscle "feel" the weight and exercise. One of the very best ways to do this is with proper form and full-range movements.

Too Much Weight

Beginners are especially prone to using too much weight. However, even advanced bodybuilders fall victim to the "heavier is best" syndrome. Heavy weights are necessary to stimulate muscle-fiber growth, but not at the expense of good form.

Not Enough Weight

Likewise, if you're not lifting enough weight, you might as well forget about stimulating new muscle growth. Muscles need overload to grow. Keep trying to lift heavier weights on a progressive basis; but again, use only good form and full-range movements.

Not Enough Rest Between Workouts

Once you've busted your butt in the gym, give your body the rest it needs. If you're still sore from your last workout, don't go into the gym just because it's your scheduled workout day. Instead, take an extra day off, and you'll be 100 percent recovered for your next workout.

Poor Diet and Supplementation

Training is only a small part of the bodybuilding equation. Eating the right combination of foods, along with good supplementation, will greatly promote your bodybuilding success. Make your diet 50 percent carbohydrate, 35 percent protein, and 15 percent fat, and take a good multivitamin/mineral and protein/carbohydrate supplement. And

don't forget the water—at least 80 ounces a day! Hydration is critical.

Not Enough Sleep

In order for your body to grow, it needs rest. That means sleep—seven to nine hours every night. Sleep is the time your body uses to repair, rejuvenate, and recover from those all-out, intense workouts. If you're not growing, you may need more sleep.

Lack of Adequate Warm-up and Inadequate Flexibility

Have you ever put a rubber band in cold water and stretched it? It quickly snapped, didn't it? That's exactly what happens to your muscles when you start working out without warming up. A warmed muscle is a more flexible muscle that's better able to lift heavier weights and work in a full range of motion. Those warmed muscles also greatly reduce your chance of training injuries.

Not Enough Intensity

One of the main reasons many body-builders train year after year without achieving any appreciable results is lack of training intensity. They're just not working out hard enough. *Raise your intensity level, and you'll increase your results.* It's as simple as that.

Too Many Sets and Reps

If your training intensity is at a high level, you won't need many sets or reps for growth. Forget those 20-sets-per-body-part workouts—that's too much. Give each body part all you've got for 3 to 6 sets *total* and watch what happens!

Stale Routines

Your body adapts very quickly to the demands placed upon it. That's why you should have a variety of exercises and routines that you use regularly. To keep your body growing, you've got to keep it off-guard. Changing your exercises and routines is a sure way to do it.

Lack of Focus

Far too many bodybuilders have no clear focus as to why they train. Sure, they say they want to stay in shape and look good, but such goals are too vague. Your mind needs clear and very specific goals to focus on.

Visualize every detail of the kind of body you want, and make concrete plans for *how* and *when* you'll achieve it. Think about those goals morning and night. Before you know it, you'll see incredible changes taking place not only in your body, but more importantly, in your attitude and behaviors, that will support those goals!

13

Hard Facts for Hard Gainers

Breaking Out of the Mold Sometimes Means
Breaking All the Rules

Bodybuilding can be the greatest thing in the world—if you're growing or getting stronger. Unfortunately, when the gains slow down, many bodybuilders lose interest or quit. During the first two years of training, the average bodybuilder can expect to gain 10 to 20 pounds of muscle. Hard gainers average about half that amount. In my book, a hard gainer is someone who's dedicated to training but able to make only slow and marginal gains at best—many times only a few pounds a year.

Just as certain body types need specific ways to be trained, the hard gainer needs to utilize many different bodybuilding success principles to reach his full potential. Let's look at some of the most important principles.

TRAINING VARIABLES

Most hard gainers are overtrained. Many of them think that if their current amount of training isn't giving them results, they should increase it. Wrong! *These people need to cut their training volume in half and double their*

training intensity! Most bodybuilders are overtrained in sets and reps and undertrained in intensity.

HIGH-REP/LOW-REP LOW-VOLUME TRAINING

The goal in bodybuilding is to keep your body off-guard and unable to adapt to the training demands placed upon it. One of the best ways to do this is by alternating your training with a combination of high and low reps. Keep the total volume of your training to bare minimum levels—just enough to stimulate growth.

Many hard gainers get great results by working their entire body no more than once in a seven-day period; some even longer, like every 9 to 12 days. For example, do one body part a day until the entire body is worked, and then take two, three, or four days off, and repeat. Maybe in one workout, you'd do a total of six sets with moderate weight for 12 to 20 reps with only 30 to 60 seconds of rest between sets. In

the next workout, you'd do 6 sets with heavy weight for 5 to 9 reps with up to two minutes of rest between sets. Each workout, you'd constantly switch the exercises, exercise order, sets, reps, weight, rest, and any other training variable that would help keep your body off-guard.

INFREQUENT TRAINING AND LOTS OF REST

This may go against regular bodybuilding dictum, but I've seen some of the best gains made by hard gainers when they train on their regular workout schedule for four weeks, then take three

or four days completely off—maybe even a day or two longer, if needed.

Another great training strategy for hard gainers is to take extra days of rest in the middle of their weekly workout schedule.

Try it. Pick any workout day, and instead of working out, take that day off. Then come back the following day and work that body part. *Force yourself to take days of rest, even when you may not want to.* Remember, most hard gainers are overtrained, and the extra rest won't hurt—in fact, it'll probably help!

REGULAR USE OF NEW ROUTINES

Get into the growth zone by using new and varied routines. Many pros change their exercises, sets, reps, poundage, and rest times every time they work

out. This is a great idea because it doesn't allow the body to get used to the same old thing. Experiment and find the best exercise, set, rep, and weight combinations for you. Then use them!

THE PRINCIPLES OF INTENSITY

One of the most important factors in growth is intensity. Raising the intensity of your workouts forces your muscles to work harder. And if you've given your body enough rest and fed it the proper nutrients, it'll grow.

Some of the best intensity principles for the hard gainer are supersets, tri-sets, and giant sets. A superset is two sets performed back to back, usually for opposing muscles—for example, a set of biceps curls followed by a set of triceps pressdowns. A tri-set is three exercises that work the same muscle performed back to back. For example, for calves you'd do a set of standing calf raises, followed by a set of donkey calf raises, then a set of seated calf raises.

A giant set is a group of four or more exercises for the same muscle. Giant sets are very intense and should be used only by advanced bodybuilders (those with at least two years of consistent training) and only sparingly.

SUPER NUTRITION SUPPORTS SUPER RESULTS

The *big* element in the hard gainer's bodybuilding success arsenal is proper nutrition. You can use the best training routines and exercises, get the right amount of sleep, and keep the stress levels down to a minimum—but if you aren't eating right, you aren't going to grow. Period!

What is proper nutrition? In a nutshell, it's eating four to six small meals daily spaced every two to three hours apart; ensuring that each meal includes 50 percent of calories from carbs (beans, rice, potatoes, pasta, vegetables, grains, fruit), 35 percent from protein (fish, chicken, turkey, lean red meat, egg whites, protein powder), and 15 percent fat; taking a good multivitamin/mineral supplement; drinking at least 10 eight-ounce glasses of water a day; ingesting 50 to 75 grams of carbs within 15 to 30 minutes after your workout; ingesting 40 to 55 grams of protein within 90 minutes after your workout.

You are what you eat. So eat the best foods, in the right combinations and at the right times, and you're bound to be successful in your bodybuilding and fitness pursuits. Use these hard-gainer strategies and watch your training take off!

"There is nothing so constant as change. Meet it. Embrace it. Enjoy it. Learn from it."

The one thing you can be absolutely sure of in your life is change. It's the only thing that never changes. The law of nature is that you either grow or you die; there's no in-between. So, what have you chosen so far? Are you growing in every area of your life? Hey, it's not enough to be growing and looking great just because you work out. That's only a small part of your life. What about your emotions, spiritual life, family, friends, career, hobbies? Are they growing as your body does? Become a complete person and not an in-shape and great-looking version of an incomplete person. There's way more to life than just working out. Go with the flow and embrace changes in all areas of your life. The change will do you good.

14

Understanding the Weider Principles for Intermediate Bodybuilders

Building onto the Foundation

In Chapter 4, we talked about the Weider Principles for beginning bodybuilders. Now it's time to discuss the Weider Principles for intermediate bodybuilders.

Muscle Priority. The essence of this principle is to train your weakest body part first in your workout, when your energy level is highest. A high degree of training intensity builds muscle, and your intensity can be great only when your energy is high.

Pyramiding. Starting with a moderate weight—about 60 percent of your one-rep max—do 8 to 12 reps as a warm-up. With each set after that, slowly and progressively increase the weight until you reach your goal of 6 to 10 reps. This pyramiding of weight allows you to fully warm your muscles, helping prevent injury while still allowing you to lift heavy weights.

Split System. The split system allows you to increase your level of intensity by training your body through various combinations. For example, you may decide to train upper body one day and legs the next, or train an upper-body part with a lower-body part. The combinations are many, but the result will always be greater workout intensity.

Flushing. You must get blood into the muscle to produce growth. Doing multiple sets for each body part causes the muscles to be flushed with blood and produces a satisfying pump that signifies that you've adequately worked the muscle.

Supersets. When doing supersets, you choose two exercises for opposing muscles (for example, biceps curls and triceps extensions), and do back-to-back sets of these exercises with little or no rest.

Compound Sets. A superset for the same body part is a compound set. A good example would be squats followed by leg extensions. Try this for an incredible pump!

Holistic Training. Your muscle cells contain proteins and energy systems that respond differently to different levels of exercise. Muscle-fiber proteins get larger when they are confronted with high-resistance loads. The cell's aerobic systems (mitochondria) respond to high-endurance training. That's why it's important that your training includes a variety of heavy/low reps to light/high reps in order to maximize your results. This is the basic tenet of holistic training.

Cycle Training.

During one part of your training year, you should construct routines for mass and strength. At other times, you should lower your weights, increase your repetitions, and train with less rest between sets (quality training). Cycle training keeps you from getting bored and helps you avoid injuries while ensuring progress in your training.

Isotension.

To practice isotension, flex a muscle you're not exercising and hold the peak contraction for three to six seconds. Do this three times per body part. Isotension can help you bring out better peak—achieve more visual details, like hardness, size, and muscle separation—through the neurological control of your muscles.

15

16 Best Barbell Exercises

The other day, a guy walked into the gym. Boy, was this dude skinny—the bulkiest thing on him was his wallet. I was resting between sets when he walked over to me.

"Excuse me," he said. "I really want to pack on some size. How long do you think it'll take?"

"This is a gym, not a place for miracles," I told him.

"I'm really that skinny?"

"I've seen more muscle on a snake," I said.

"What can I do?" he asked. "I'm tired of being thin."

I assured him, "Listen, you've come to the right place. The most important thing you can do is heavy barbell training. That's the way you can add mass."

"What exercises should I do?" he asked.

"Do those that build the foundation. I call them bodybuilding's greatest barbell exercises. They're the ultimate for building strength and mass."

With wide eyes and a big grin, he said, "I'm really into mass!"

"Hey, we'll talk religion later," I said. "For now, you need to learn the exercises."

TO BEGIN

Start off with an overall warm-up. For each exercise, do a specific warm-up of 1 to 2 light sets before using your training weight (one heavy enough to make you put forth a big effort to complete the higher number of reps). Always use excellent form in resistance movements.

THE EXERCISES

Standing Curl (Biceps)
If you're tired of your puny arms being bruised from your shirt sleeves slapping against them, this exercise is for you. In a standing position, grip the bar slightly wider than shoulder-width, and keep your elbows locked at your sides. Curl until the biceps are peak-contracted.

MASS TIP: Use a close grip to hit the outer biceps and a wide grip to hit the inner biceps. Do 3 sets of 5 to 9 reps.

Reverse Curl (Biceps, Forearms)
If you think a brachialis is something found in your throat, do this exercise.

Standing curl (a)

Standing curl (b)

Your brachialis muscle is under your biceps. Instead of an underhand grip like you use on the barbell curl, take an overhand grip. Keep your elbows close to your sides. Do 3 sets of 7 to 11 reps.

MASS TIP: Try "21s" to really feel the burn from the start through the finish. On the first 7 reps, go only to midpoint. The next 7 reps, go from midpoint to finish. Do the final 7 reps nonstop from start to finish.

Bench Press (Chest)

If your upper body resembles a bony frame covered with skin, start benching. Keep your body flat on the bench. Grip the bar slightly wider than shoulder-width, and inhale as you lower the bar to your lower chest. Keep your elbows close to your sides throughout the movement. Exhale as you press the weight up.

MASS TIP: The closer you bring the bar to your neck and your elbows back to shoulder level, the more you'll feel it in your upper chest. Do 3 sets of 8 to 10 reps.

Incline Press (Chest)

This exercise is similar to the bench press, except you use an incline bench

to target the upper chest. (Or is it the bony area just below your neck?) Do 3 sets of 8 to 12 reps.

MASS TIP: The closer your hands are to the center of the bar, the more you'll feel the exercise hit the center (vertical separation) of your chest.

Close-Grip Bench Press (Chest, Triceps)

Start with the same body and elbow position as on the bench press, but

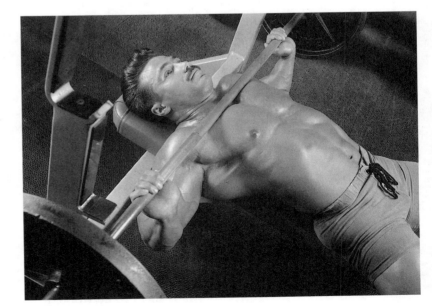

Bench press

bring your hands in so they're six to eight inches apart. Lower the bar and press up to full lockout. Do 3 sets of 10 to 15 reps.

MASS TIP:

For extra intensity, do 3 to 5 short-range lockout reps at the end of your set. Straighten your arms completely, then lower the weight only one to two inches and lock the arms and contract them forcefully. You'll be amazed at how much this will burn!

Overhead Press (Shoulders)

If the clothes hanger from the cleaners is wider than your shoulders, overhead presses will change that. Do these either standing or seated, in front of or behind your neck. Take a slightly wider than shoulder-width grip and, in a controlled manner, lower the bar behind your neck to the upper trapezius (or the upper-clavicle area, if you prefer pressing from the front). Keep your elbows pointed down, not back. Do 3 sets of 8 to 12 reps.

MASS TIP: To make those deep fibers contract, take four seconds to lower the bar—contracting the deltoids the entire time—and with a quick, explosive movement, press the weight up.

Upright Row (Traps)

So you think traps are something you set for mice? Uhhh . . . no. We're talking about the trapezius, a large muscle that covers the top and back of the shoulders and extends down to the middle of the back. Upright rows will work the upper trapezius, building a thick wall of muscle above your shoulders. Take a shoulder-width overhand grip. Keep the bar close to your body and raise it up to about chin level, making sure to elevate your shoulders. This will make the traps do the lion's share of the work.

MASS TIP: The closer the grip, the more directly the traps seem to be worked.

Upright row (a)

Upright row (b)

Conversely, the wider the grip, the more you'll feel it in the deltoids. Lower the bar under control until your arms are fully extended. Do 3 sets of 9 to 15 reps.

Deadlift (Back, Legs)

No, it isn't what you'd do at a funeral. This fantastic exercise will work your lower back, traps, glutes, and legs. Proper form is crucial. Choose which of these two grips you prefer: the over/underhand grip (hands shoulder-width apart, one hand over and the other under) or the double overgrip (traditional overhand grip, but with hands rotated slightly forward and over the bar).

Place your feet about shoulder-width apart. Keep your arms locked and fully extended. Squat down until your thighs are about parallel to the floor. Keep your back tight and your head up and looking forward. Your chest should be slightly forward and over the bar.

Straighten your legs and raise the weight off the floor. Keep the barbell close to your legs throughout the movement. As your legs get closer to full extension, straighten your back to the upright position. Do 3 sets of 4 to 6 reps.

MASS TIP: Take an extra minute or two of rest between sets so you keep excellent, injury-preventing, mass- and strength-producing form while using heavy weight. For a different type of intensive workout, use lighter weight and keep your rest periods no longer than 45 to 60 seconds between sets.

Stiff-Legged Deadlift (Hamstrings)

Same as the deadlift, except you do this exercise on a platform for a greater stretch, and your legs remain in a nearly locked-out position (knees slightly bent) from start to finish. The key to feeling this in your hamstrings and glutes is to not round your back. Keep the back tight and slightly arched. Do 3 sets of 6 to 9 reps.

MASS TIP: Be sure to lower the bar as far as you're comfortably able. For some, the bar touches the tops of their shoes.

For others, this may be slightly below knee level. The important thing is to feel the stretch and keep the bar close to the body throughout the movement.

Squat (Quads, Glutes)

You say your legs are so thin they could double as letter openers? Say no more—you need squats. Forget all those fancy machines; if you want serious jeans-busting quads, squats are king!

Here's how to do back squats (although I prefer front squats). Stand under a squat rack and rest the bar at a comfortable spot on your traps. Keep your feet about shoulder-width apart, turned slightly out. (Keep your legs and feet together if you want to add more outer-thigh sweep.)

With a slight arch in your lower back and your head up and looking straight ahead, squat down until your thighs are about parallel to the floor. Always make sure your knees travel in a direct line over your big toes. For more stability, you may want to slightly elevate your heels. Do 3 sets of 6 to 10 reps.

Wide-Stance Squat (Inner Thighs)

To target the inner thighs, perform the squat as described above, but with a wider stance. Keep your legs about three feet apart and turn the feet outward (always making sure the knees travel in line over the big toes).

Wide-stance squat (a) and (b)

Hack squat

Hack Squat (Quads, Glutes)

This is a real quad burner if you do it right. Most bodybuilders don't; they keep the bar away from their glutes instead of holding it right up against them throughout the entire movement.

Elevate your heels slightly, and keep your upper body erect. Position the bar against your lower glutes where they join the upper hamstrings. Squat down until your thighs are about parallel to the floor.

Come back up, but don't lock out; keep constant tension in your quads. For more power and less knee stress, keep your legs about 8 to 10 inches apart and your feet pointed straight. One more thing: do nonstop reps. If you want burn, this will do it! Do 3 sets of 10 to 15 reps.

Bent-Over Row (Back)

If a banana has wider lats than you, you need rows! The row is a classic exercise that will work your lats (latissimus dorsi, a large muscle that covers the middle of your back).

With an over-hand grip, start with your legs slightly bent, and lean forward at the waist. Take a slightly wider than shoulder-width grip and bring the weight up into your midsection and pull your arms back. Lower the weight until the arms reach full extension. When you pull the weight up, focus on making the back contract. Be sure to pull your arms back and the weight into your waist. You should feel a big difference between the two movements.

Because they can't see their backs contracting, most bodybuilders neglect

Bent-over row (a)

Bent-over row (b)

Bent-over row (c)

this important growth and strength component. Feel the back contract and work! Do 3 sets of 5 to 9 reps.

Shrug (Traps)

This isn't what you do when you're confused—it's another great trap builder. Most bodybuilders do shrugs with the bar in front of the body. Take a shoulder-width grip, keep your arms locked, and shrug your shoulders straight up (don't roll them) toward your ears.

MASS TIP: For variation, try this with the barbell behind you. Take an overhand grip with your palms facing to the rear. You won't be able to use as much weight, but you'll feel the movement differently. Do 3 sets and keep your reps in the 5 to 7 range.

Wrist Curl (Forearms)

If Popeye was your hero, you're probably a good candidate for building big forearms. One of the best exercises to do so is the wrist curl. Rest your arms on a flat bench, firmly anchoring your wrists—with the palms up—just slightly over the edge of the bench. Don't move them throughout the exercise. Relax your wrists, then bring your hands up as you curl the weight toward your forearms. Do 3 sets without counting reps—go for the burn, all the way to failure.

MASS TIP: For a burn that's out of this world, curl the weight to full contraction, then uncurl it about one inch and curl to full contraction again. Keep this going until it becomes impossible to move the weight at all.

Reverse Wrist Curl (Forearms)

Do this movement like the wrist curl, except with an overhand grip. This really smokes the top of your forearms. Again, do 3 sets and don't count reps—do as many as you can.

MASS TIP: Follow the same mass tip guidelines as with the wrist curl. This, too, will give you a pump unlike anything you've felt!

A FEW WORDS ABOUT REPS

Some training articles in books and magazines give a standardized number of reps for a particular exercise and mode of training. For example, 3 to 5 reps for power, 6 to 12 reps for mass, and 15 to 20 reps or more for greater pump, definition, and endurance.

For the majority of bodybuilders, this system works fairly well. However, in this chapter, I present a different set of rep ranges for two different reasons:

1. Through trial and error and talking with many bodybuilders all over the world, I found these rep schemes to be superior for the given movement.

2. You will better remember a specific exercise when you're given an unusual rep scheme like 5 to 9, 7 to 11, or 9 to 15, as opposed to the usual 8 to 10 reps per exercise. It's one thing to read about an exercise and quite another to remember all the nuances. I want you to get the best results; if it takes a weird rep scheme (that works!) to make it happen, then consider it done.

"If you do anything long enough, you're bound to get good enough."

It's true. When you start working out, you feel so overwhelmed, because not only is there so much to learn, but it's easy to believe that everyone else in the gym is in better shape than you. Well, I've got news for you. Even the most in-shape person started at the same place you did—as a beginner. We all have to start there. The incredible thing is what kind of person you become when you stay on the fitness and bodybuilding road long enough to really start enjoying the ride. I guarantee that if you'll be patient and stay the course, you'll be awesome much sooner than you think.

11 Best Dumbbell Exercises

Years ago, I knew of an old man who lived alone on a farm in a rickety shack just on the outskirts of town. His friends called him John; others called him huge. With a back nearly as wide as a drive-in theater screen, arms like clubs, a chest that resembled an armor plate, and delts the size of cantaloupes, John was still quite a specimen at 70 years of age.

When the local muscleheads came by to watch John train in his old horse barn, many were surprised to see that he used only dumbbells. You see, John was living proof that dumbbell-only training produced incredible results. Yet it wasn't so much the dumbbells, it was how he used them.

Of course, John didn't do every exercise every workout, nor did he work the whole body every time. Rather, he mixed things up: two or three exercises for 3 to 4 sets each per body part each training day worked well. As an observer, let me share with you John's favorite dumbbell exercises.

Row (Back)

When you looked at John from the side as he stood with his arms relaxed, his lats added about four inches to his width. When he turned around and spread those wings, his back flared like the hood of a cobra.

John's back exercise of choice was the row. It gave him greater range of motion and increased ability to more strongly contract the hits. He always did rows with his opposite knee on a

Row

Flye (Chest)

A slight incline on the bench gave John just the right amount of stretch and complete fiber stimulation. He chose a weight he could do perfectly for 8 to 10 reps. Holding a dumbbell in each hand and arms locked out above his chest, John crossed his legs so that he wouldn't cheat by exerting too much downward pressure or overly arch his back.

At the top of the movement, he never let the dumbbells touch, and he kept only a slight bend in his elbows as he lowered the weights until the dumbbells were about chest level. He told us that as he raised the weight, he'd imagine he was putting his arms around a big barrel, maintaining that position until the weights were directly overhead. This visualization helped him do the movement correctly.

flat bench and his other leg slightly bent, his foot firmly planted against a six-inch wooden platform.

He'd lower the weight as far as possible to stretch his lats, then bring his elbow back and the weight up until his hand was even with the side of his upper torso. John lowered the weight farther than most bodybuilders, but ensured the shoulder was stabilized and never allowed it to hyperextend. He did 8 reps per set.

Pullover (Chest, back)

John preferred doing this movement across a flat bench. He kept his arms straight throughout the range of motion and his glutes well below the bench; only his middle and upper back came into contact with the bench. John extended his head and neck off the edge of the bench, tilted slightly back.

He reminded us that breathing was important: take a big inhale when

Pullover (a)

Pullover (b)

the weight is at the top and being lowered, and a powerful, forced exhale when bringing the weight up from the bottom position. For the best stretch, John lowered the dumbbell until it was only inches above the floor and then, with arms still locked, brought the weight back up and over his head to the starting position. As far as reps go, the big man always did 20.

Bent-Over Lateral Raise (Shoulders)

John told us that this was the best exercise for widening out, and he liked to begin his delt workout with it. Rear

Bent-over lateral raise (a)

Bent-over lateral raise (b)

delts, he said, were the slowest to grow and should therefore be worked first. John placed a towel over the top end of an incline bench on which to rest his forehead. With arms slightly bent, he raised the weights up and away from his body, turning his thumbs down. He worked in the 12- to 15-rep range.

Arnold Press (Shoulders)

To John, presses for shoulders were like squats for quads: often difficult, but always growth-producing. He did them a number of ways: standing, seated, and with a twist (popularized by Arnold Schwarzenegger years ago). To do the Arnold press, he told us to keep the upper torso firmly erect and supported with either a bench or a belt to stabilize the shoulders.

Since this movement is more difficult than regular dumbbell presses, John went a bit lighter on the weight. He always started the exercise with his arms to his sides and palms facing in. As he pressed the weight up, he simultaneously turned his wrists until his palms faced forward. He cautioned us that elbow positioning is a bit tricky: keep the elbows pointing directly out to the sides and in line with the upper torso as the weight is raised; keep them pointing downward and never back or forward when the weight is lowered. He did 6 to 12 reps per set.

Kickback (Triceps)

John took what many bodybuilders today consider to be a finishing movement and made it a mass builder simply by changing the weight and technique. First, he did a few high-rep warm-up sets, then slowly added weight and decreased the reps each set. He leaned forward at the waist, keeping his upper arm firmly against his side.

The real difference was his elbow position—he kept it slightly elevated, higher than his back, to make his triceps work more. At the top of the

Kickback (a)

Kickback (b)

movement, he pronated his hand, which contracted his triceps even harder. John did 20 reps for his warm-ups and 6 for the heavy sets.

Lying Extension (Triceps)

This is similar to the lying French press done with an EZ-bar. John lay on a flat bench with his feet crossed and his head slightly off the end of the bench. With a dumbbell in each hand, he brought his upper arms back and toward his head at about 45 degrees.

Keeping his elbows in that position, John lowered the weight, then extended back up to full lockout. He did 6 to 12 reps.

Scott Curl (Biceps)

Can we talk guns? Big John had two of the biggest I'd ever seen. Dumbbells, he explained, gave him the best stretch, degree of rotation, and range of motion. Scott curls were his favorite movement.

He said that with strict attention to form, this exercise would give the

Lying extension (a) and (b)

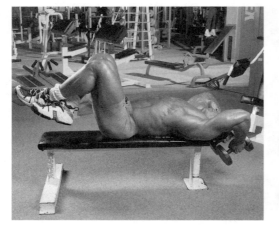

Scott curl (a)

Scott curl (b)

biceps greater fullness at the point of the lower attachment. He told us to keep the entire upper arm against the incline pad and to slowly lower the weight until the arm is fully extended—but not hyperextended.

John preferred doing one arm at a time for better isolation and concentration. He also urged us to keep our biceps contracted throughout the range of motion and not let them relax by curling the weight too far back toward the shoulder. He did 5 to 7 reps with heavy weights and 12 to 20 with lighter weights.

Thumbs-Up Curl (Biceps brachialis)

John did this movement to add biceps fullness and brachialis development. (He said his old training buddies used to call them hammer curls.) He kept the weights down at his sides with his thumbs up, then curled the weight up, keeping his thumbs in the same relative position. As the weights reached chest level, he'd supinate his hands, turning his wrists up. John's upper arms didn't move. He preferred doing 9 reps.

One-Legged Squat (Legs)

Big John was blessed with good genetics in the leg department, but that didn't mean squat unless he worked them hard. Doing farm chores like pushing a full wheelbarrow didn't hurt. But to John, mass was one thing, shape another. He never counted reps, but we did. He did no fewer than 12 one-legged squats (lunges) and sometimes as many as 50.

John used heavy dumbbells with enough weight to call them squats. He held the dumbbells at his sides or up next to his shoulders (like doing a press, only with palms facing). The emphasis was on form and making the quads burn by doing nonstop reps— none of that "rest at the top and then go down again" stuff.

He emphasized the importance of keeping the knee in a direct line over his big toe during the exercise to prevent injury. He went down below parallel; he said it gave him better shape, sweep, and development.

The quad of his nonworking leg always stayed in a direct line with his upper torso; never in front or behind.

Stiff-legged deadlift (a)   **Stiff-legged deadlift (b)**

Stiff-Legged Deadlift (Hamstrings)

Having great quads is one thing; having great hamstrings is quite another. Besides picking up hay bales and feed sacks, John improved his hamstrings with this exercise. First, he always stood on a wooden platform that was at least six inches high, which gave him a better stretch.

At the top of the movement, he held the weights at his sides. As he leaned forward, his arms and the dumbbells rotated forward—yet always stayed close to the legs—until his palms faced his shins at the bottom of the movement. John kept his back slightly arched, his head up (in line with his upper back) and his knees slightly bent. He told us to lower the weight only as far as the hamstrings were fully yet comfortably stretched. Sets of 6 reps gave him all the results he wanted.

17

22 Best Machine Exercises

Machines were designed to make our lives easier, but do they make them better?

Easy isn't necessarily something you're after if you're an experienced bodybuilder. Some individuals choose machines because they follow fixed grooves—it's hard to go wrong when it comes to form, which is especially good for beginners.

Some newer brands closely mimic freeweight movements, a real plus. While I don't have space to list every machine available and the top brands, I'll give you the 22 best exercises using the basic machines you'll find in just about every health club.

A word to the wise: use machine training as a change of pace, not as the foundation of your workout program. Choose a few different ones each work-out; change the weight, reps, sets, rest, and other variables. Watch and talk to advanced bodybuilders to learn the subtle technique variations that machines allow to better target your muscles.

SMITH MACHINE

This popular machine has been hot for quite some time. It approximates the feel of a barbell, but travels within a fixed groove and goes only straight up and down. Here are some of the best exercises you can do:

Shoulder Press, Incline/Decline Press, Flat Press (Chest)

Keep your elbows wide (pointed away from your upper body) and straight up and down, not forward or backward.

Wide-stance squat

Squat

Try high-rep sets (don't lock out) and different hand spacings every 3 reps within the same set.

Squat (Quads)

The Smith machine is especially good for wide-stance squats with your feet pointed out to hit the inner thighs. Place your heels 6 to 12 inches in front of you; notice the difference in feel. For wide-stance squats, keep your legs and feet directly under the bar. For all squats, make sure your knees travel in a direct line over your middle toes, but don't extend beyond them.

Row (Back)

This is a good exercise with which to use strip sets. After you do 6 reps, have a spotter take some weight off each side, then do 4 more reps. Repeat this one more time, and rep out until you reach failure.

CABLE STATION

Whatever happened to the good ol' cable station that had its own weight stack, operated smoothly, and had adjustable pulleys? Lots of us wish they were back because the arm, delt, and chest exercises you could do on them were incredible. Yet all is not lost. Today's cable machines—some even use rubber belts in place of cables—offer good alternatives to those "lost" exercises of the past.

Crossover (Chest)

For a different feel, do your reps leaning forward at the waist and in line with the weight stacks, almost mimicking a most-muscular pose.

Flye (Chest)

For a true feel, position the bench—incline, flat, or decline—so that your arms, hands, and the cable are in a direct line with the center of the weight stacks.

Flye (a) and (b)

Curl (Biceps)

The closer you are to the low pulley, the harder the initial pull and subsequent tension throughout the movement. Likewise, if you stand away from the pulley, the same weight will feel lighter.

Pressdown (Triceps)

Regardless of what bar or rope you use, position your body close enough to the weight stack so that the cable travels in a direct vertical line—not at an angle— throughout the range of motion. This will work the triceps harder.

Upright Row (Traps)

Keep your body positioned far enough away from the low pulley so that the angle between the machine weight stack and the cable forms a V as you pull. Use nonstop reps of 12 or more and descending sets for a major pump.

Lateral Raise (Quads, Glutes)

Use a low swivel pulley and experiment with body proximity—close and far, left and right—to the weight stack to emphasize different areas.

Lateral Raise (Shoulders)

Try this movement with the cable behind your back. For rear delts, use both high pulleys and pull across your body.

Lateral raise (a)

Lateral raise (b)

Vertical Leg Press (Quads, Hamstrings)

To smoke the inner thighs, do adductor presses. Keep your legs perpendicular to the foot platform and use a wide stance, turning your feet out 20 to 30 degrees. Lower the weight and bring your legs out to the sides of your body. Squeeze the inner thigh muscles as you push the weight back up.

Lying leg curl (a)

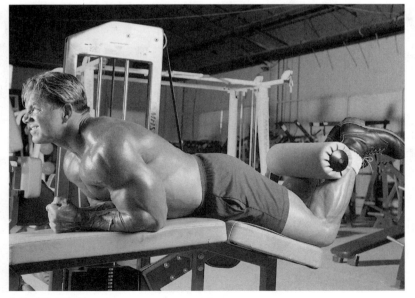

Lying leg curl (b)

45-Degree Leg Press (Quads)

For an extra contraction, lock your knees and rock back on your heels as you push to full extension, allowing your toes to rise off the platform.

Lying Leg Curl (Hamstrings)

Rest your forearms on the bench under you to elevate your upper body. As you curl your legs, drive your hips into the bench, which will isolate the hamstrings as well as protect your lower back.

Seated Leg Curl (Hamstrings)

For a greater stretch, lean forward throughout the entire movement.

Supported Leg Curl (Hamstrings)

Instead of leaning forward and using the forearm pads, keep your torso upright. Don't rest between sets.

Hack Squat (Quads)

For more frontal thigh sweep, keep your legs and feet close together and raise your hips away from the back pad. Keep the area from your knees to your shoulders in a straight line. Only your traps and shoulders should come into contact with the back pad throughout the exercise.

Seated Calf Raise (Calves)

Lean forward so that your upper body is over your knees to feel a greater calf burn.

PULLDOWN MACHINE

The pulldown is that good ol' machine with the weight stack in front of you and the bar attached to a cable above you.

Front Pulldown (Back)

For a better contraction, use a reverse grip. Keep your back slightly arched and your elbows far behind you in the bottom position.

Seated calf raise (a)

Seated calf raise (b)

Curl (Biceps)

Lie on a flat bench with your head directly underneath a high cable and pulley while holding a short bar attached to the high pulley. Keep your upper arm at 90 degrees and curl the bar toward your face. Slowly return to the fully extended position. Go for high reps, peak contraction, and the burn.

Preacher Curl (Biceps)

Keep your elbows close and your grip wide. Always fully extend your arms before doing your next rep.

"Take an action to create a reaction."

To many people, taking action means picking up the phone and ordering the latest infomercial gadget that promises incredible results and rarely delivers anything near it. Sorry folks, but taking action to have the body you want means getting off your butt and doing something about it. It means making a choice to eat better and work out regularly. It means that you let your mouth stop talking about it and let your body do the talking for you, with the incredible results you've achieved from doing the basic things that build beautiful, in-shape bodies. If you don't get started, it's absolutely certain you won't arrive—so get started and stay started until you reach every goal you want to achieve.

18

All About Superset Training

My blood rushes through me like a raging river. My chest swells like a balloon. My back feels as wide as a drive-in theater screen. I've never felt such a pump and muscle tightness. And it's all because of one training technique (among many) that my good friend Joe Weider named years ago—the superset principle.

Want to know what superset I did to achieve this physical nirvana? Barbell incline presses to wide-grip pull ups. That's it—boom, boom, baby, one exercise after another, with about 30 seconds of rest in-between. But there's more to it than just doing two exercises back to back. You've got to know form, function, exercise sequence, and combinations.

SO, WHAT THE HECK IS A SUPERSET?

Supersets simply involve taking two exercises (not for the same muscle group—those are called compound sets) and performing one after the other with minimal rest. Biceps and triceps are great body parts to superset.

The possibilities are endless: seated dumbbell curl to lying EZ-bar French press, barbell curl to close-grip bench press, cable curl to kneeling overhead French press with a cable, and the list goes on.

WHY DO IT?

Because it works. Doing one exercise after another with minimal rest saves time, increases training intensity and the amount of blood going to your working muscles, and provides an aerobic effect.

Get used to the fact that if you're supersetting, you won't be able to use nearly the amount of weight you would if you were doing straight sets. Not a problem. The superset intensity level will more than make up for that.

HOW OFTEN SHOULD I SUPERSET?

About every fourth workout. Use the other three workouts to accomplish your strength and mass goals by emphasizing more straight-set, heavy-weight

GREAT SUPERSET ROUTINES

Imagination is what you need to create effective superset routines tailored for your body. Here are a few to get you started.

Quads to Hamstrings
- Leg press to lying leg curl
- Squat to barbell stiff-legged deadlift
- Hack squat to standing leg curl

Quads to Calves
- Leg press to seated calf raise
- Hack squat to reverse hack-squat toe raise

Chest to Back
- Incline barbell press to wide-grip pullup
- Decline press to reverse-grip barbell row

Back to Chest
- One-arm dumbbell row to straight-arm dumbbell pullover
- T-bar row to incline dumbbell flye

Back to Delts
- Seated cable row to bent-over dumbbell lateral raise
- Behind-neck pulldown to dumbbell lateral raise

Biceps to Triceps
- Seated dumbbell curl to lying EZ-bar French press
- Strict barbell curl (back against wall) to dip

Triceps to Biceps
- Dip to simultaneous dumbbell thumbs-up curl
- Reverse-grip pressdown to hammer curl

Abs to Lower Back
- Crunch to back extension
- Hanging knee raise to modified dumbbell stiff-legged deadlift

Hack squat

Standing leg curl

One-arm dumbbell row

Straight-arm dumbbell pullover

Reverse-grip pressdown

Hammer curl

Crunch

Back extension

training. Yet play it by ear. If you don't have much energy on a day when you intend to go heavy, do supersets.

HOW MANY REPS PER BODY PART SHOULD I DO?

Since you're using lighter weights, do more reps. I recommend the following reps for these body parts: chest 9 to 12; back 10 to 15; shoulders 12 to 15; biceps 9 to 12; triceps 12 to 20; quads 15 to 30; hamstrings 10 to 15; calves 10 to 20.

HOW MANY SUPERSETS SHOULD I DO?

Of course, everyone's body responds to superset training in a unique way. You may need more or fewer sets and reps depending on your goals, genetics, level of training experience, mental ability to generate intensity, nutritional factors, and recovery ability. As a general guideline, however, a beginner with four

months of straight-set training can get good results from two supersets per body part; an intermediate, after nine months of training, could do three to four supersets per body part; and advanced bodybuilders with more than 18 months of training can do five to six supersets per body part.

WHAT KIND OF RESULTS WILL I EXPERIENCE?

After the second or third superset, you'll feel a terrific pump in both body parts you're working. If not, you need to increase the intensity level of each movement by either using more weight and fewer reps, less weight and more reps, faster reps, or decreasing rest time between exercises.

Most bodybuilders who've used supersets report feeling bigger and fuller. They also say they feel more in tune with their muscles and experience an increased ability to generate a greater muscle pump when they go back to doing straight sets.

19

Accessories for Growth

For the love of easy gains, wouldn't it be nice to go to the gym, do a few exercises, go home, eat, rest, and grow? But you know it takes more than that for sizable gains. Even if you have the right exercises, diet, and supplementation in order, sometimes the body needs a little extra boost—*not drugs*, of course, but training accessories.

As proven intensity uppers, these accessories can help you lift more and give you far better training results, each in its own way. Some should be used regularly. Others should be used sparingly. Let's look at these accessories, their pros and cons, and the best exercises to use them with.

Belts

Belts are probably the most widely used bodybuilding accessory. They help increase back support by upping abdominal wall pressure. The more tightly you cinch the belt, the greater the abdominal pressure against the spine, which thereby helps support the spine and keep the entire torso tight, maximizing both strength and safety.

You'll find a variety of belts: thin leather, thick multilayered leather for powerlifting, and nylon mesh with an inflatable back bladder. The great thing about the inflatable bladder is that it can be custom-fitted to the curvature of your lower back. Leather and nylon mesh can't, and that can be an important factor if you're looking for the best fit and maximal support.

Cost: $20 and up
Best uses: Squat, deadlift, overhead press

Gloves

Ever get calluses or blisters on your hands from all those workouts? A popular solution is lifting gloves, which give your palms just enough padding to minimize calluses and help prevent slippage. You'll find them in leather, mesh, or nylon, or any combination of the three.

An important factor to consider is hygiene. Let's face it—many gyms leave a lot to be desired when it comes to cleanliness and germs. You just never know who used the weights before you, or whether the individual was sick.

Gloves minimize exposing yourself to those risks. Nevertheless, be sure to regularly wash your gloves—and hands.

Cost: $10 and up
Best uses: Any pressing, pulling, or curling movement

Straps

One of the best ways to develop forearm strength is to progressively use heavier weights without using straps. However, once you reach the point when your grip strength begins to limit the amount of weight you can use, you should use straps.

Straps can help accelerate your muscle and strength gains by allowing your arms to act as hooks to lift the weight. Many times, you reach grip failure before reaching muscle failure on the muscle you're training. Straps prevent this. Equally important, straps, by allowing you to loosen up on your grip, help take unwanted and often limiting muscles out of a movement (such as the forearms on pullups, pulldowns, rows, and shrugs).

Straps come in a variety of materials, such as cotton and nylon; and narrow, medium, and wide widths. Many bodybuilders prefer the wider straps simply because they don't dig into the skin like the narrow ones can.

And don't forget about straps with hooks. These are great, because all you have to do is position the hook over the bar and lift—no wrapping the strap around the bar and making sure it's tightened before you lift.

Cost: $6 and up
Best uses: Back exercises, including one-arm dumbbell row, deadlift, bent-over row, pullup, and barbell shrug

Wraps

Wraps are to the knees what straps are to the wrists—support when weights get heavy. Like straps, wraps are best used on maximal or near-maximal lifts and should not be used as a crutch.

Powerlifters have this wrap thing down pat. Their focus is on developing strength and explosive power unaided (without wraps) until they get into the *really* heavy sets. Then, wraps are used for only a few sets at most and usually for no more than 5 reps per set.

You'll find a number of wraps on the market; the most popular is the Superwrap. Be sure to get wraps that are thick and tightly elastic. And when storing your wraps, don't roll them—fold them. This will help keep their elasticity longer.

Cost: About $18 a pair
Best uses: Squat and deadlift

Chalk (Magnesium Carbonate)

Not too many years ago, chalk was as common in gyms as barbells and dumbbells. If a gym was a *real* gym, it had chalk. Why? Because chalk was and still is a big help for serious lifters. Nowadays, many gym owners won't put chalk in their clubs because it might turn off or intimidate prospective members—or, heaven forbid, certain parts of the gym might get a little dusty. Please!

Think about how many times your grip felt slippery while holding that barbell or dumbbell. And how many extra reps could you have done if your grip had been more secure? A little chalk on the palms and fingers could have prevented that.

Chalk also helps you get psyched up. There's something special about getting those heavy dumbbells ready or preloading a heavy barbell and walking over to the chalk box to rub some of the stuff on your hands.

Cost: At about $8 for a one-pound box, chalk is a lifter's bargain!
Best uses: Press, row, curl, deadlift, shrug, and squat. Yes, squat! A little chalk on the bar where it rides across your back and on your T-shirt or sweatshirt across your traps will help prevent the bar from slipping during the exercise.

Powerlifter Inhalant (Smelling Salts)

I mention this one not so much as an endorsement, but rather as something you might want to consider occasionally. You've probably seen on television when smelling salts are given to someone who needs to be revived. It really works. (If it doesn't, the person is probably dead.)

Years ago, some wrestlers, powerlifters, and bodybuilders started using smelling salts to help them get psyched up for big events. I've used them sparingly only on my heaviest lifts—usually squats and deadlifts—and they definitely increased my mental awareness. But a note of caution: don't inhale too long or too often. A quick inhalation—one second or less—in each nostril is all you need. And if you're going to use it, do it only on your heaviest lift.

Cost: Varies
Best uses: Squat, deadlift, leg press, bench press

Towel (Bar Wrap and Partner Pull)

And you thought your towel was for wiping off sweat! Here are a few other uses:

- Try wrapping the squat bar with the towel where the bar rests on your back. This will help keep the bar from digging into your back, letting you focus on the quads during the exercise and not on the bar.

- Don't forget partner-assisted towel pulls. They're a great way to finish a back or arm routine. For your back, sit on the floor facing your partner with your partner's feet against yours. Each of you grab one end of the towel (use a hand towel and not a bath or beach towel). Have your partner pull the towel until you reach a maximal lat stretch. Then, you do the same. Do 15 to 20 reps.

- A hand towel can work great for curls and French presses, too. For curls, stand with your arms close to your sides and hold the towel with your forearms parallel to the floor and hands spaced about six inches apart. Have a partner grab the towel ends and apply resistance as you curl the towel up. On lowering, resist his force on the way down. Keep the arms moving throughout the exercise.

- Finally, stand or sit as you hold the towel behind your head. You may want to keep your hands next to each other, or one hand above the other (as if grabbing a rope) and simply rotate the hands in order to feel each triceps work maximally. Have a partner apply firm yet controlled resistance from top to bottom of the exercise. Go for the burn and do at least 15 to 20 reps.

"It was the only thing he knew and it was the only thing he became."

I can't tell you how many people I've seen year after year who do the same thing over and over and over and never change the way they look and feel. Then, they innocently ask why they aren't getting better results. Duh. The reason they stay stuck in the rut year after year is because they want to stay right where they are—and don't you dare believe otherwise. It doesn't take a rocket scientist to know that if an exercise or diet is not bringing great results, one must change it and keep changing it until she finds the things that work best for her. Of course, we know that'll never happen to you now, will it? I'd better see your head shaking up and down for a big yes!

20

Winning Diet Strategies

Get Big, Firm Up, and Live Long

Diet. I don't know about you, but most folks are just plain turned off by the word. I've always wondered—is diet something you do, or is it what you eat? Whatever the case, the failure rate for people who diet is abysmal. With so many experts in the field and so much information available on the subject, why do we mortals fall short of our weight-loss (it should be fat-loss) goals?

One reason may be the lack of a specific plan. Apply real-world-tested information on a ready and able body, however, and the result is bound to be successful. To help you achieve that end, three of the best fitness, body-building, and longevity experts will share with you how to build up, shape up, and live long, healthy, and fit. See if you can guess who the experts are.

TIPS ON REDUCING AND SLIMMING

Not all carbohydrates are the same. Starchy carbs are potatoes, rice, pasta, greens, and cereals. Fibrous carbs include most vegetables and some fruit. Eat starchy carbs in the morning (no later than 2 P.M.) and fibrous carbs in the afternoon, and don't eat a lot of refined sugar (also a carb).

Remember to eat every three hours. Many people think they have to eat a full meal every three hours, but it's better to "graze" by eating small amounts of nutritious food throughout the day. You could even eat seven to eight small meals a day.

Drink a protein supplement as a substitute for one or two of those small meals. For example, you could have a good breakfast of eggwhites and oatmeal, then have a protein drink three hours later.

When you don't have time to prepare a bowl of rice, half a potato, chicken or any other nutritious food, grab a drink instead. We're all busy— the most important thing is to make nutrition work for you.

And don't freak out, thinking you can't have a few lowfat potato chips with that half of a tuna sandwich. Just eat small amounts and keep everything in moderation! After 2 P.M., eat only protein, fibrous vegetables, and maybe an apple.

Get your protein from tuna, any kind of white fish, chicken breast, turkey, lean beef, eggwhites, and protein powder. Be sure to take a good multivitamin/mineral supplement with breakfast. During my workout, I drink an electrolyte-replacement drink that contains vitamin C, magnesium, manganese, zinc, and potassium.

Here's my sample diet:

Meal 1: (Breakfast): 4 eggwhites, 1 egg yolk, small bagel

Meal 2: Bowl of rice or protein drink

Meal 3: Salad with one can of tuna, lowfat dressing, baked corn chips

Meal 4 (last major carb meal—about 2 P.M.): Potato, yam, protein drink

Meal 5: Lowfat cottage cheese, apple

Meal 6 (Dinner): Fish or chicken, green vegetables

Meal 7 (Bedtime snack): One cup of tea

TIPS ON GAINING MASS

Eating one gram of protein per pound of body weight per day is a good guideline. Eat five to six small meals throughout the day to help your body better absorb the nutrients. You need some fat in the diet, but keep it less than 15 percent of your total caloric intake.

The variable factor in all of this is your carbohydrate intake, which will make up the remainder of your daily calories. The exact number of grams depends on your size, training level, experience, and metabolism. Stick with complex carb sources like rice, pasta, oatmeal, and some breads, with simple carbs from fruit. Good protein sources include chicken breast, skinless turkey, lean cuts of beef, eggwhites, and a good whey- or egg-based protein powder.

Here's what I recommend for the hard gainer:

- Vary your protein sources with each meal.
- For breakfast, have 6 to 10 eggwhites with 1 to 2 yolks, oatmeal, 1 to 2 pieces of whole-wheat toast and fruit.

- For the next four to five meals, have a different lean protein along with two different complex or fibrous carbs. You can substitute a protein shake for one to two of these meals.
  - Be sure to take a good multivitamin/mineral supplement with breakfast.
  - If you have the extra money to supplement, try taking amino acids right after training. I prefer branched-chain amino acids.
  - Drink as much water as you want during the day.
  - If you have no digestive problems, you can eat a small protein meal up to one hour before bedtime. I always try to eat a protein meal late at night—even before a contest—and have found that if I missed that meal, I don't sleep very well.

DIET WISDOM FOR THE OLDER ATHLETE AND VEGETARIAN BODYBUILDER

The biggest problem for older athletes is that they don't eat enough. They slack off, their energy level is low, and they don't get enough protein. I suggest eating one gram of protein for every two pounds of lean body mass per day. This protein should come from the food you'd normally consume rather than a supplement.

Older athletes should also consume more fat and fewer carbohydrates. Fat burns more slowly than carbohydrates and protein; and since most athletes aren't eating enough calories each day, the added calories from fat will help increase their total daily caloric intake.

A hard-training younger athlete may consume 65 percent of calories from carbs, 25 percent from protein, and 10 percent from fat. Reducing the carbs by about 10 to 15 percent and increasing the fat calories by the same percentage will give the older athlete more energy by providing a fuel that will last a longer time.

Ideally, eating small, frequent meals throughout the day is the best way to get nutrients. Many older athletes are so busy, however, that eating three meals a day is a chore. More protein, fewer carbs, and higher fat seem to solve the frequent feedings and energy problem.

Athletes on a vegetarian diet usually have different nutrition goals than athletes who want to get big and strong or have a 19-inch arm. Those on lacto-ovo or vegan diets are generally more concerned with longevity and health. Vegetarian athletes tend to minimize their intake of processed foods and eat more whole grains, vegetables, and fresh fruits. Here's a sample of my diet:

Breakfast: 3 to 4 poached eggs, lowfat cottage cheese, 2 to 3 pieces of whole-grain bread, fresh fruit (not juice)
Lunch: vegetable soup, beans and rice
Dinner: soufflé or textured protein (similar to a meat patty), baked potato or yam, large salad, fresh fruit

I believe in taking supplements, but not in megadoses like 1,000 times the RDA. Taking too much of a supplement can overtax the body's ability to use it and flush it out of the system. I take a good multivitamin/mineral along with extra vitamin C and bioplasma salts.

I'm a firm believer in drinking lots of water, and I drink at least eight or nine big glasses a day. When you look at how much water the body contains, dehydration probably causes more problems than bad dieting.

21

Knowledge Is Power—If It's Used

Expand Your Muscles with Your Mind

Bodybuilding—nothing to it, right? Just throw a few weights around and watch those muscles grow. Hardly. Much of modern bodybuilding is based on cold, hard scientific fact. To get anywhere in the sport requires that you know what you're doing. And for many, learning about bodybuilding is a neverending process.

More than 50 years ago, when Joe Weider started writing about training, very little (if any) bodybuilding and sports nutrition information existed. Most bodybuilders relied on word-of-mouth aphorisms, anecdotes, and old wives' tales passed from gym to gym.

Today, it's a different story. Over time, bodybuilders have dramatically increased their knowledge about training and nutrition. Thanks to *Muscle & Fitness* and other cutting-edge magazines, gaining practical, scientific bodybuilding knowledge requires only a trip to a newsstand or your mailbox.

Fortunately for the aspiring physique champ, the education doesn't stop there. Let's explore some of the other valuable sources for acquiring bodybuilding knowledge.

SEMINARS—LEARNING FROM THE PROS FIRSTHAND

One of the best ways to gain training knowledge is through seminars. Many gyms throughout the country hold training and nutritional seminars for the benefit of their members and the general public.

There's nothing quite like listening to your favorite pro in person as she shares the training secrets and nutritional advice that led to victory. It's like having a professor in sweatpants giving you a graduate course in iron! The amount of information you can pick up is incredible. As a sage once said, "Spending a half-hour across the table from a wise man is worth more than a month's study of books." So very true!

SHOWS—KNOWLEDGE PLUS INSPIRATION

Bodybuilding and fitness shows are a great source of training information and inspiration. Many of the people who go to these shows are serious bodybuilding and fitness enthusiasts. They have a wealth of knowledge to share.

Common at many of these events are product exhibition booths. These booths offer a great opportunity to talk to people in the fitness industry about the latest trends, products, exercise techniques, and nutrition science. Take advantage of the situation and chat with some of these experts. Then go and watch the show and get fired up!

BOOKS—JUDGE THE BOOK BY ITS WRITER

Walk into any major bookstore and check out the health and fitness section. You'll find title after title of training, nutrition, and conditioning books. With so many to choose from, which one should you buy? Yes, my friend, when you bought *Bodybuilding 101*, you did buy the right book! Congratulations and thank you.

However, for all those other books you might want to buy, I strongly suggest going with an author who has solid credentials and a track record of success. Pick someone whose expertise is in the subject you're interested in. Stay away from those who make outrageous promises and claims that sound too good to be true (they probably are).

VIDEOS—GAINING FITNESS FROM YOUR VCR

Many people don't have time to go to fitness shows, bodybuilding contests, or seminars. And reading can be a long and laborious process. In fact, research has shown that the majority of people who buy books never read past the first chapter! And even if they do read, some people have trouble applying information from books to their training programs. What's a bodybuilder to do?

Go no further than your VCR. Many top pro bodybuilders and fitness experts make and sell videos of their routines and philosophies, including such topics as training for mass, shape, cuts, power, nutrition, and supplementation. Videos on aerobics, cardiovascular health, and even stretching are also available.

Having a video allows you to carefully study exercise technique and the nuances that can make a difference. And seeing the routines in action makes them easier to copy. Also, you can watch it at your leisure—even in slow-motion, to really get it right.

AUDIOTAPES—"EARS" A GOOD WAY TO LEARN

Almost everyone has access to an audiocassette player. Maybe that's why an increasing number of bodybuilders are listening to cassette tapes on training, nutrition, and motivation to pump up their routines.

Audiocassettes have many advantages. You can listen to them while driving, or when doing mundane tasks like cleaning the house. You can also put them in your portable cassette player and listen to them at the beach, during long walks, or even when you're at the gym.

Some people simply assimilate information more effectively when listening to cassette tapes. One reason for their effectiveness may be that the subconscious mind records everything it hears. After you hear the message enough, it begins to sink in.

Of course, you learn a lot by simply working hard in the gym. As long as you work out safely, trial and error can be an excellent teacher for how to best work your body. Use your mind as you build your body. The results will be worth it.

"Know the difference between adequate and optimal."

I'm telling you, this distinction will make all the difference in what you get out of life. Far too many people only do what is adequate to get by—like get unimpressive results or not get fired. But why would anyone want to do that, when they could experience tremendous rewards by giving a little more effort? Never settle for the quick fix or miracle cure, because the most successful people in all walks of life will tell you that they don't exist. You won't experience great things just by doing enough to get by. Great people do great things and accept nothing less in everything they do. So I ask you, do you feel great?

PART III

Secrets That Will *Really* Change Your Body

22

Advanced Bodybuilding

A One-on-One Routine for the Experienced Bodybuilder:
Goals, Expectations, Weights, Proper Form, Nutrition

You're bustin' your butt in the gym, and you've made some great gains. You've been on a beginner program (for a minimum of four months) and intermediate program (for at least five months), and by now you've got a good understanding of the basic movements. You've established your own workout style and have set workout goals based on the body you want. You now know which body parts grow quickly and which don't.

After nine months of training, you've had some exposure to intermediate intensity training principles. And if you're like most intermediate bodybuilders, these principles have helped produce some dramatic changes in growth and strength. Now it's time to learn the training principles and philosophy of an advanced bodybuilder.

DOING LESS TO GAIN MORE

A strange bodybuilding phenomenon occurs after you've been training for about six months—the rate of growth slows down. When you began

bodybuilding, your body grew and seemed to change overnight. Talk about excitement! Yet after you continued to train and get stronger, your body grew, but not nearly as fast. In fact, you probably had to work more to get less. That's no fun.

But they say patience is a virtue, and this is never truer than in bodybuilding. A lot of people quit once those incredibly fast gains start to slow down. For most bodybuilders I've talked to, strength and muscle mass gains slowed down the most after three years of conventional sets-and-reps training.

However, when those same lifters reduced the number of sets, exercises, and training days and increased the rest time between workouts, muscle mass and strength continued to go up steadily—regardless of how many years they had been training.

What these successful bodybuilders discovered was that as they grew stronger, their ability to generate an effective workout intensity increased. In other words, it took less time to produce better workouts. Instead of taking 12 sets to fatigue the chest, they could now do it with 6 or less.

It's important to note two things. First, less workout time is needed to produce better results. Second, any effort beyond that which is required to stimulate growth and strength is considered overtraining. For the smart bodybuilder it all boils down to experimentation. For some, if 6 sets can stimulate growth, what about 4? If 4 sets can do it, how about 3 all-out sets?

THE IMPORTANCE OF FORCED REST BREAKS

If you, as an advanced bodybuilder, can now generate greater power and inten-

sity much more quickly, then your workouts should be better and take less time. The question is, what do you do with all that "free time" away from the gym? Rest and enjoy your life!

The greater physiological demands in intense training require that you give your body more rest. Hard workouts tax your central nervous system, along with your muscles and connective tissue. World-record bench presser Ken Lain (he can regularly bench over 700 pounds!) once told me that his body needs 21 days to recover after an all-out lift.

I know some weight trainers who think they're ready to hit the iron and work the same body part again two days after a hard workout. "I'll lose strength and get small," they tell me. Not so. *The truth is, they'll get small and lose strength because they haven't allowed enough time for recovery!*

I caution you not to wait until you stop growing, stop getting stronger, or have an injury before you take a layoff. Take an extra day off from training any time your body is still sore from a previous workout. And take a complete week off from training every six to eight weeks. If you think you'll get weak or out of shape, don't worry—you won't. Remember, you control your body. Your body doesn't control you unless you give it that power!

THE ADVANCED WORKOUT

I could write a whole book full of advanced workouts, but that wouldn't help you find the workouts best suited for your body type, genetics, goals, and level of commitment. So would you settle for one good one to get you going in the right direction? Good— here it is.

THE ONE-ON/ONE-OFF, TWO-ON/TWO-OFF PROGRAM

All Training Days

Stationary bike (5-minute general warm-up)

Stretching (10 minutes)

Day 1

Exercise	Sets	Reps
Quads		
Front squat (shoulder-width stance, feet pointed slightly outward)	3	6–10
Leg press (feet wide and pointed out)	3	8–12
Sissy squat	2	to failure
Hamstrings		
Lying leg curl	3	10–12
Stiff-legged deadlift (use dumbbells one workout and a barbell the next; pyramid the weight, making your last set the heaviest)	3	6–8
Calves		
Tri-set the following exercises in this order:*		
Standing calf raise (heavy)	3	5–8
Machine donkey calf raise (moderate)	3	9–12
Seated calf raise (light)	3	12–20

*You must go nonstop from one machine to another. Rest no longer than 45 seconds between tri-sets.

Day 2

Rest

Day 3

Exercise	Sets	Reps
Chest		
Incline dumbbell press	4	6–8
Flat bench dumbbell press (compound set with)	3	8–10
Close-hand push-up	3	to failure

Front squat (a)

Front squat (b)

Stiff-legged deadlift (a)

Stiff-legged deadlift (b)

Seated calf raise (a)

Seated calf raise (b)

continued on next page

THE ONE-ON/ONE-OFF, TWO-ON/TWO-OFF PROGRAM *(continued)*

Day 3 (continued)

Exercise	Sets	Reps
Back		
Chin-up (wide-grip)		
(compound set with)	4	to failure
T-bar row (close-grip)	4	8
Seated cable row	3	8–12

Day 4

Exercise	Sets	Reps
Delts		
Bent-over dumbbell lateral raise	4	12–16
Seated barbell press (wide-grip)		
(compound set with)	3	12
Standing dumbbell side lateral		
(light weights with very strict		
nonstop reps)	3	20
Traps		
Shrug (alternate barbells and		
dumbbells each workout with)	3	5–8
Cable upright row (close-grip with		
straight bar)	2	12–20
Triceps		
Lying EZ-bar French press		
(compound set with)	4	8–10
Pressdown (straight bar)	4	16–20
Biceps		
Standing barbell curl (do drop sets,		
working heavy to light)	5	15,12,10,8,6
Lying dumbbell curl (lie on your		
back with upper arms at a 45-degree		
angle away from bench)	3	10–15

Day 5
Off

Day 6
Off

Chin-up (a)   Chin-up (b)

Standing dumbbell side lateral (a)   Standing dumbbell side lateral (b)

Standing barbell curl (a)   Standing barbell curl (b)

THE NUTRITION OF AN ADVANCED BODYBUILDER

To give you a quick review without delving into specific nutrition requirements for the endo-, ecto-, or mesomorph, let me just make a few nutritional observations for any advanced bodybuilder.

- Eating four to six small meals per day, every three hours, works well for increased metabolic response and optimum nutrient absorption and utilization. Be sure each meal consists of roughly 50 percent calories from complex carbs, 35 percent protein, and 15 percent fat.

- The postworkout drink and meal are critical for maximizing your bodybuilding gains. Be sure to have a carb drink (at least 50 to 75 grams of carbs) within 30 minutes after your workout. Have a high-quality protein meal with 40 to 55 grams of protein within 90 minutes after training.

- The following supplements should be considered if you really want to maximize your training gains. In order of importance, they are:
  1. Vitamins and minerals
  2. Protein/weight-gain powders
  3. Creatine monohydrate (note: creatine works well for some people and not so well for others)
  4. Branched-chain amino acids (BCAAS)

The Lowdown on Creatine and Aminos

Good research data have been reported on the benefits of creatine monohydrate on muscle storage of creatine phosphate, though far more long-term studies are needed to truly evaluate its effectiveness. Creatine has been shown—at least short-term—to help increase energy for greater muscular contractions and strength. And creatine can help draw water into your muscle cells, which, of course, translates into bigger, fuller muscles. Always look for 99 percent pure creatine monohydrate. Follow label instructions.

Another supplement I recommend is branched-chain amino acids, or BCAAS. If you train hard and your diet lacks sufficient protein or carbs, your body may be forced to feed off its own

lean tissue—that's right, your own muscle tissue—for sustenance. It can do this because three amino acids found in muscle can be used for energy.

To counter this, many bodybuilders supplement with BCAAs. Many of the top pro bodybuilders tell me they use BCAAs before and after their workouts. You may want to experiment and see if they can work for you.

And, of course, don't forget the water! You should drink at least 80 ounces each day. Replace those soft drinks, alcoholic beverages, and coffee with pure, clean water. Hydrate your cells all day long. You will feel the difference, and your body will love you!

GOING BACK TO OLD ROUTINES THAT WORKED

Remember that training log I told you about? Well, the more advanced you get, the more you'll find yourself going back to it for routines that worked. In fact, you'll find that using beginning and intermediate workouts alternately with your advanced training will produce excellent gains.

Forget about going heavy all the time. For growth and strength without the wear and tear on the body, you simply don't need to. Cycling your workouts with excellent beginner, intermediate, and advanced routines will pay the greatest bodybuilding dividends.

TIPS TO HELP YOUR BODY GROW AND GET STRONGER YEAR AFTER YEAR

Weak-Point Training
Every 10 weeks, pick a body part that you would like to improve. Train that body part—and no other—every day for seven days. At the end of the seven days, take five days off from working that body part. After the rest period,

resume training the body part using your regular routines. This will allow one week of specific-body-part-only training for each of the five major muscle groups (chest, back, legs, shoulders, and arms) in a one-year period. A great way to jump-start some serious gains!

Weak-Link Training
Want to blast out of the training rut? Do weak-link training. Specifically, train the weakest point in any given exercise. For example, let's say your squat poundage won't go up. What can you do? Two things: first, use a power rack, adjust the rack pins, and do sets of quarter- and half-range movements. Second, without using the power rack, do a regular squat, but stop each rep at the bottom position for two seconds, then come back up and repeat.

These dead stops will give you incredible power from the bottom position. You can also do power-rack and dead-stop training on presses and deadlifts with equally great results. I suggest doing dead-stop and power-rack training once every two weeks.

Single-Exercise, Heavy-Basic Movements
A good beginner program will allow you to make consistent, excellent gains. As an advanced bodybuilder, going back to single-exercise, heavy-basic movements will work wonders after you've been doing workout after workout of multiple exercises, isolation movements, cables, and so on.

Simply pick one basic movement for each body part. Use only that exercise on the day you train that body part. Do 6 sets of 6 reps, but go heavy. Do this every sixth workout and watch what happens!

Fluctuating Reps
You know by now that if you constantly shock the body with new exercises, sets, reps, weights, rest periods, and angle

combinations, you will grow. No two ways about it. Play around with different rep variables in your workouts.

In one workout, go heavy and do triples (3-rep sets). Next workout, go light and do high reps with minimal rest between sets. *Always change the variables in your training. Never, ever do the same thing twice.*

A FINAL WORD

You probably know someone who has decided to get bigger, stronger, and leaner faster by getting on "the juice." Yeah, I mean steroids, GH (growth hormone), IGF-1, clenbuterol, and whatever else is the current rage.

Years ago, bodybuilders were interested in basically one thing: bodybuilding. They experimented and developed new exercises, routines, and nutritional strategies that gave them great results without drugs. They did it all *naturally.* Being striated or having 6 percent body fat wasn't what real bodybuilding was about. It was a lifestyle, a philosophy, almost a religion, and a way to be healthy—both inside and out.

It's quite a changed scene now. Sure, the majority of bodybuilders train and get great mass and strength results naturally. But for those who choose drugs, it's mental torture to see themselves get incredibly huge and strong so fast, only to know that if they want to continue to be that big and strong, they've got to stay on the drugs indefinitely. I've seen this lead to drug addiction and many other problems.

So many potentially great bodybuilders have given up or have become permanently injured because of what the drugs have done to them. That's only the tip of the iceberg. You wouldn't believe the mental hell, ruined relationships, bad business decisions, and spiritual deprivation these people experience. Not to mention that possession of these drugs is a punishable felony in the United States.

What many also fail to realize is that a large percentage of these drugs on the market are counterfeit, with no active ingredients. These people are playing Russian roulette, because no one knows for sure what substances they really contain! Can you imagine putting stuff into your body and not knowing what it is?

It's time for this to stop! We've got to get back to what this sport has always been about—*pure bodybuilding*. We must become experimenters and trailblazers again. To be different from everyone else. To not be like sheep. To take a stand and be able to look at yourself in the mirror each night and say, "Yes, I did the very best I could today, and I did it naturally." Only then will you be able to believe that you are a rare person indeed—*a real bodybuilder*!

23

Growing About It the Right Way

Variations on a Theme

Being in shape is a great thing. Not only do you look better, you feel better too. Though the benefits of fitness are universal, how you get in shape is a very individual thing. With so many options (weight training, biking, hiking, racket sports, walking, running, aerobics, swimming, and so on), picking the best workout program for your needs can be confusing.

The bodybuilding lifestyle just might be the best choice for your fitness goals—especially if you want to change the look of your whole body. Can you do it? You bet you can. The following is a list of the basic exercises for specific areas that can help you build a new you.

CHEST

To fully develop the chest, you'll need to hit three different areas: the lower, middle, and upper pectorals (pecs). Exercises like flat and decline benches and dips work the middle and lower pecs. Presses done on an incline bench work the upper chest and fill in the area near the clavicles. Finishing move-

ments like flyes and cable crossovers hit the inner chest and help give the entire chest more shape, cuts, and refinement.

BACK

For back width, nothing beats chin-ups for spreading the scapulae and hitting the lats. Done either in front of or behind the neck, with or without weight, chins are a terrific way to get that wide, tapered look.

For middle- and low-back thickness, don't neglect rows. Rows can be done many ways: seated with a low cable pulley; bent over with a barbell, dumbbell, or cable or on a T-bar platform; or lying on an incline bench.

To hit the lower back and spinal erectors, be sure to include deadlifts in your routine. Keep your regular heavy deadlift work to once a week.

SHOULDERS

If you want big, thick, meaty caps on your shoulders, do presses. They can be done either seated or standing, with a

machine or with freeweights, held in front of or behind the neck. To blast rear delts, do bent-over dumbbell or cable laterals. If you want wide shoulders, concentrate on side laterals with cables or dumbbells. If your front delts are lagging, add a set or two of front delt raises with dumbbells, a barbell, or cables.

Traps can be hit with upright rows or shrugs. Upright rows are best done with a barbell or cables, while shrugs can be done with a barbell, dumbbells, cables, a Smith machine, or a bench press machine.

BICEPS

One of the very best ways to pack on biceps mass is with standing curls,

using a barbell, dumbbells, cables, or a machine. With curls, the variations are nearly endless. Doing dumbbell curls seated on an incline bench works the long belly of the biceps muscle called the brachialis.

Concentration curls with a barbell, dumbbells, or cables give the biceps more peak. The important thing is to *feel* how each of the exercises affects your biceps growth, and adjust your training accordingly.

TRICEPS

For overall triceps mass, weighted dips, French presses (lying; seated; or standing with a machine, a barbell, dumbbells, or cables), and close-grip bench presses can't be beaten. For refinement and shape, triceps pressdowns with a bar or rope are favorites of many bodybuilders.

Simply changing the kind of bar you use affects the emphasis on the triceps heads. Using a straight bar or a rope hits the triceps' middle and inner heads. A curved bar, held with your arms locked to your side or bent over with arms extended above your head while standing, really hits the long outer head.

QUADS

Someone asked me which exercise I would choose if I could do only one exercise for the entire body. I answered that without a doubt, it would be squats. They are not only the king of all leg exercises, but they simultaneously work other body parts (back, shoulders, abs, arms) as well.

Squats can be done with a barbell; or on a Smith machine with the bar placed across the front delts, upper chest, or clavicles, or on the back across the rear delts. You might want to place a block under your heels for added balance or to emphasize more quad above the knee.

The hack squat, done on a machine or with a bar resting under and against the glutes, is another great way to hit the quads. Leg presses, either vertical or at a 45-degree angle, blast the quads with a greater emphasis on the ham/glute tie.

For a finishing movement, do leg extensions either on a flat seat for mid- to lower-quad separation or on a decline for upper-thigh separation. Experiment and vary your foot positioning to hit the inner thigh (toes in), middle thigh (toes straight), and outer thigh (toes out).

HAMSTRINGS

Filling out the hamstrings won't be a problem if you use a variety of exercises like leg curls—either standing, seated, or with a cable that has an ankle strap—stiff-legged deadlifts, and back extensions. You don't need to do all of these exercises on the same day. Try a few in one workout and others in the next. A little trick that will help you feel more of the movement is to keep your toes pointed down when doing leg curls.

CALVES

Big and shapely calves really stand out. The following exercises can help turn your calves into cows!

Standing calf raises are great at hitting the gastrocnemius and the entire calf muscle. Seated calf raises are good at stressing the soleus and giving the calf greater thickness. Donkey calf raises on a machine or free-standing with a partner are another excellent way to blast the overall calf muscle, especially the inner calf. Try high-rep toe raises on a leg press if you want a calf pump and burn that's out of this world! Be sure to vary your toe positions to hit the inner, middle, and outer calf heads.

ABS

The abs can be worked with a number of exercises. I'd like to offer you two that will hit your midsection and lower abs: crunches and hanging leg raises. Crunches are a great way to hit the overall ab muscles. Keep your arms in front of you (not behind your head) when you do these to minimize the chance of neck strain and injury.

Hanging leg raises hit the lower abs. By raising your knees from side to side, you'll hit the intercostal and serratus muscles more. Remember: it's important to bend the torso to fully contract the abs.

Use these exercise variations to give your muscles more variety and intensity for strength and growth. The body adjusts very quickly to whatever demands are placed upon it. To keep it growing, you've got to keep it guessing, and one of the most effective ways is by constantly changing the order and the kind of exercises you do each workout. Most importantly, have fun in your training. It'll help keep you growing and growing.

"The more you think about what you don't have, the more you create what you don't want."

You need to know a little something about that incredible thing between your ears called your mind. It's like a loyal servant who will help you get anything in life, if only you give it the right commands (think the right thoughts). Now, this servant doesn't question whether what you tell it is right or wrong. It simply accepts what you believe as true and then works on giving you the new habits, actions, attitudes, and beliefs that match perfectly to the commands you've been giving it (commands you probably never knew you were giving it). The more you think about what you *don't* have, the more you create that very same condition in your life you've been trying so hard to avoid. The solution? Think only of the things you *do* want!

24

When Cheating Is the Right Way

And Other Advanced Weider Principles

Earlier in the book, I told you about understanding the 13 Weider principles that are specifically designed for beginning and intermediate bodybuilders. Joe Weider gave bodybuilders a lexicon of terminology they could understand when it came to getting the most out of their bodybuilding training. The Weider principles, as Joe and millions now call them, are designed to give bodybuilders a systematic approach to achieving optimal results in weight training.

In this chapter, we'll take a look at the advanced Weider principles— 19 techniques that can help propel your training to new and greater dimensions.

Cheating. Using good form is imperative in getting the most out of your workouts. However, still greater results can be obtained by slightly cheating in the movement a few times after you've completed the majority of reps in good form. Used sparingly, this principle can help break sticking points.

Tri-Sets. Doing three exercises for the same muscle group without a pause is called a tri-set. Hitting the muscle from three angles makes this more of a shaping movement, yet it will give you a tremendous pump.

Giant Sets. A giant set is a series of four to six exercises—with little or no rest in between—for one muscle group. By repeating the series three to four times, you'll hit the muscle completely.

Pre-Exhaustion. Pre-exhaustion is when you work a muscle group to the point of fatigue in its primary motion using an isolation movement, then immediately superset that exercise with a secondary motion using a basic movement. A good example would be pre-exhausting the quads by doing leg extensions, followed by squats.

Rest–Pause. To use rest–pause, do as much weight as you can for 2 to 3 reps, rest for 30 to 45 seconds, squeeze out another 2 to 3 reps, rest 40 to 60 seconds, do another two reps, rest 60 to 90 seconds, then finish with 1 to 2 more reps. You will have done a long set of 7 to 10 reps near max. Skeptical? Wait until you try it!

Peak Contraction. Peak contraction is keeping full tension in a muscle when it's in the fully contracted position. Keeping constant tension in your muscles helps to peak and striate them.

Continuous Tension. Many bodybuilders train so fast that they swing their weights through most of the range of motion. This decreases the amount of work the muscle actually does, and increases the possibility of injury. Training slowly and deliberately with constant tension makes the muscle work harder and increases intensity.

Reverse Gravity. This involves resisting the downward force of your weights as you lower them. This very intense form of training produces a great deal of muscle soreness and is an excellent way to stimulate maximum muscle growth. Reverse gravity (negative) training should be done only occasionally.

Forced Reps. Forced reps should be used after you've completed as many reps as you can on your own. Have a training partner help you complete one or two forced reps. This is an intense form of training, and forced reps work well when used sparingly.

Double-Split. This principle allows you to work one or two body parts in the morning and another body part in the evening. This gives you more energy and intensity for each workout, thereby increasing your overall training intensity.

Triple-Split. This principle involves training three times a day, working a different body part each session. This is for bodybuilders who have tremendous recovery rates.

Burns. When you do 2 to 3 short partial reps at the end of your regular set, you bring extra blood and lactic acid into the muscle you're training. This increased lactate causes discomfort known as *burns*. This helps contribute to the size and vascularity of the muscle.

Quality Training. Quality training means that you gradually reduce your between-sets rest time while doing more repetitions than usual (or as many as usual).

Descending Sets. Known as "stripping" by many bodybuilders, this principle is just that—the gradual reduction of weight within the set of an exercise. For best results, have a training partner strip the weight so you can continue to keep training with very high intensity without stopping and changing the weights yourself.

Instinct. Only you know what works best for your body. That's why it's important for you to do the exercises, sets, reps, and workout schedule that allow your body to grow.

Eclectic Training. Combining mass-building and isolation-refinement movements into a specific training system is *eclectic training*. Choose a variety of movements and general principles that work best for you.

Partial Reps. As a means of increasing power and size, you can do partial reps at the beginning, midpoint, and finish position of exercises. You can use much higher poundages when doing partial reps, which greatly strengthen the muscles and connective tissue.

Speed. This principle advocates the use of heavy weight in strict, controlled form. However, instead of concentrating on how slowly you lift the weight, explode off the bottom of the movement as quickly as you can. As the weight becomes harder to lift, keep trying to explode with the weight more and more rapidly.

Staggered Sets. This principle calls for staggering your smaller, slower-developing body parts between sets for larger muscle groups. A good example would be doing a set of wrist curls between a set of squats. This allows your weaker body part to be trained without taking away from the primary muscle group you're training.

GETTING THE MOST OUT OF BODYBUILDING

Joe Weider designed the Weider principles to help you reach your bodybuilding goals in the shortest time possible. Wise and careful use of these principles can help bring you the results you seek. Be patient, and don't try all of these principles at once. Gradually introduce each new principle into your workout routine. And be sure you are using techniques that are appropriate for your training level.

Longevity is the name of the game when it comes to staying in great shape. Train intelligently, and you'll continually reap the incredible benefits of the bodybuilding lifestyle.

25

Get Unstuck

Variation Gives You Freedom to Grow

Have you reached a sticking point in your workouts? Or do you just want to add a little more vitality to your training? Many times, a slight variation in exercises, sets, reps, rest, and angles is all it takes to get back in the groove for fitness success. In this chapter, I'd like to give you some training variations that will bring you good and consistent results.

VARIATIONS IN ROUTINE

Regularly creating and using new routines will keep your workouts fresh and enjoyable. Just the idea of trying something new helps us look forward to our next trip to the gym. Here are two new routines for you to try:

Four-On/One-Off

With this routine, you split the body into four separate groups and work those groups on certain days for four days in a row and then take one day off. Here's how it looks:

Day	Body Parts
1	Chest, side delts, calves
2	Hamstrings, triceps, abs
3	Back, rear delts, calves
4	Quads, biceps, abs
5	Rest

Three-On/One-Off, Three-On/Two-Off Split

This popular routine divides the body into separate groups but works them all in a three-day period. Also, it allows for one day of rest the first time through, then two days of rest after the second sequence. After two days of rest, you simply repeat the three-on/one-off, three-on/two-off cycle. Here's how it looks:

Day	Body Parts
1	Chest, side delts, triceps, abs
2	Back, rear delts, biceps, stationary bike
3	Legs, calves

VARIATIONS IN SETS AND REPS

Doing the same number of sets and reps every workout is a sure way to become stale and halt your training progress. Try using these set-and-rep variations and watch what happens!

Ten Sets of 10 Reps

Ten sets of 10 reps is an intense way of working the muscle for maximum growth. The keys to making 10 sets of 10 reps work are: take only one basic exercise for each body part, use heavy weight with good form, and do exactly 10 sets of 10 reps. (Squats and pullups work extremely well with this arrangement.)

Be prepared for a tough workout. You'll need more rest between sets, but that's okay. After you've completed the 10 sets of 10 reps, don't do any further work for that muscle! I suggest using 10 sets of 10 reps no more than once every three or four weeks.

Heavy–Light Routine

This set-and-rep combination takes one body part and works it with two exercises done back-to-back. For example, for biceps do a set of heavy barbell curls for 6 strict reps. Put the barbell down and pick up a pair of moderately heavy dumbbells, then do one set of super-strict thumbs-up hammer curls for 9 reps. Do a total of 3 back-to-back sets. Get ready for a fantastic pump!

Variations in Angles and Rest

Angles *do* make a difference in how thoroughly you work a muscle. Varying exercise angles allows you to work all parts of the muscle belly—low, middle, and high attachments. Hitting all areas helps ensure more symmetrical and complete development.

When you work a muscle with heavy weight, you naturally need more rest for the muscle to recuperate for the next set. Sets with heavy weight impose specific recuperative demands, and the rest time between sets shouldn't be rushed. Training with lighter weight and higher reps doesn't require as much recuperation between sets.

Try using a combination of moderate weight and higher reps with brief rest periods along with the heavy-weight, low-rep work. This not only keeps the body off-guard against new and varied stimuli, but helps develop all-around strength and conditioning as well.

"Follow your conscience, no matter how hard it may seem at the time."

You'll never go wrong if you let your conscience be your guide. Hey, when it comes to making decisions about things in your life, all you have is your awareness right now. Make the best decision you can with the awareness that you have. Later on, when you get more awareness, you'll be able to make a different decision if necessary. For now, at this time in your life, the best decision you can make is always the right decision for you and for your growth and learning. Never forget that. Always be your best friend and stop being so critical of and hard on yourself. Best friends unconditionally accept you for who you are, and so should you.

26

Formulating New Routines

Practical Advice That Will Keep You Growing

One of the greatest benefits of working out is the feeling you get from seeing your body change. Gaining more muscularity, strength, and hardness is enough to keep any bodybuilder pumped up for the long haul.

But, after a few years of working out, some bodybuilders reach a plateau, and the gains stop. This leads to frustration, causing some to quit. Unfortunately, many of these frustrated individuals opt for the quick fix for strength and mass by taking steroids and the like. What a big mistake! So how do you keep progressing, even if you hit a nasty plateau? The answer may be as close as a pencil and a notebook.

THE MAGIC OF A TRAINING LOG

Keeping a training log, a detailed record of your workout routines, is a great way to help you get past sticking points. A log will enable you to formulate new and varied routines so you can enjoy great training success for many years.

It's simple, really—just keep a record of every workout you do. This is important for a number of reasons:

1. A log gives you a good indication of your training progress. If you're getting stronger, your body will show it.
2. A training log gives you precise information as to which exercises are working and which aren't.
3. This valuable feedback allows you to keep the exercises that work for *your* body and eliminate the ones that don't.
4. You can refer to your training log at any time and formulate new routines from the set, rep, and weight combinations that work best for you.

For years, the best bodybuilders in the world have used training logs. Think about it: can you remember a workout you did four months ago that got your legs incredibly sore? You could if you looked it up in your training log. Enough said.

IT'S ALL ABOUT EXPERIMENTATION

The second element of your long-term bodybuilding success is exercise experimentation. If you want to grow, you've got to do the exercises that make *your* body grow. That doesn't mean doing what the person next to you is doing just because it looks cool. You've got to become your own exercise scientist.

You can try numerous exercises for each muscle group. Some will work well, and others won't do diddly. Instead of taking someone else's word for it and copying his routine, go to the gym and find out for yourself what works!

Many times an exercise won't produce results until you change the *angle* of the movement—then it becomes an incredibly effective growth and strength producer. However, you wouldn't have discovered and benefited from this unless you took the time to test every element of the exercise. You must search for every part of an exercise that works for you and you alone!

APPLYING WHAT YOU'VE LEARNED

The third element of real bodybuilding success is exercise application. This means taking those exercises that work best for you and applying them in ways that will give you long-term results.

As you may have found out, your body can quickly become stale. If you keep doing the same exercises and routines month after month and year after year, you're not going to grow to your greatest potential.

You must keep your body off-guard. How? By using different combi-nations of exercises, sets, reps, and weight, and by increasing intensity. Instead of doing only straight sets, mix it up and do supersets (two exercises for opposing body parts, for example, triceps and biceps), tri-sets, and giant sets (multiple exercises performed back-to-back for the same body part).

You might decide to pick one exercise for one body part and do 10 sets of 10 reps. How about doing two different exercises for a body part and doing a heavy–light superset? For example, do heavy standing barbell curls for 8 reps, then immediately do a set of dumbbell hammer curls for 12. This combination will help you build biceps mass and peak. Performed correctly, it's a killer!

The exercise variations are endless. You're limited only by your imagination. If you're serious about getting the most from your training on a long-term basis, you've got to find the best exercises for you, mix them up regularly, write those workouts down in your training log, and refer to the log often in order to formulate new exercise routines.

The most important reason to train is to have fun. Enjoy your workouts. Enjoy how wonderful your body feels after a good workout. Most of all, enjoy the priceless and precious gift called your life! Bodybuilding isn't something you *have* to do. To get the most from bodybuilding, it should be something that you *want* to do. Follow these guidelines, and you'll enjoy many years of looking and feeling great!

PART IV

Specialized Training for Your Body Type

27

Training for the Endomorph

Better Gains for Bigger Bods

One of the questions most asked by bodybuilders is *How should I train?* As you can imagine, coming up with one answer is a challenging task. We all have different body types, goals, levels of experience, motivation, training time, nutritional needs and habits, and other factors.

Since what works best for one person may not work for another, I will present some practical training advice based upon one particular aspect: body type. In this chapter, I'll discuss training for the endomorph (the kind of body that tends to be heavyset) in greater depth.

While many of the exercises I discuss will work for any build, it's *how* you do them that can make all the difference with regard to your body type.

THE TRAINING PHILOSOPHY

Endomorphs typically have a higher than normal percentage of body fat. On the plus side, many endomorphs are blessed with a big and wide bone structure. Weight gains come easily, and losing body fat is much more difficult.

Many times, the weight endomorphs gain stays right where they don't want it—on the abs, waist, and buttocks. As endomorphs begin weight training and bodybuilding, they tend to gain size—much of it muscle—fairly quickly. However, it often remains hidden under layers of fat. Ironically, an endomorph's body can be hard as a rock, yet achieving a good degree of definition always seems just out of reach.

Many endomorphs, because of their advantageous bone size and ability to put on muscle quickly, train with heavy weights and low reps. Often, this is a mistake. An endomorph should train with moderate poundage, high intensity, minimal rest between sets, and more frequent workouts. The goal is to amp up the metabolism, make the muscle burn, and carve new cuts and definition.

Another *very* important training element is cardiovascular fitness. Far too many endomorphs simply do weight training and nothing else, and that's another big mistake. An endomorph will never achieve the degree of leanness she desires unless she has a good diet and trains her cardiovascular system at least three times per week. Excellent cardiovascular workout choices include brisk walking (regular or treadmill), stairclimbing, biking (road or stationary), racket sports, and hiking.

Be sure to do your cardiovascular training in the target heart rate zone, a range that is dependent on your age. To compute your target heart rate range per minute, subtract your age from 220 and multiply that number by 0.6 and 0.7. After a five-minute warm-up, exercise in your target heart rate zone for 15 to 20 minutes, then cool down for three to five minutes.

THE WORKOUT

Let's keep the workouts fun. That means changing your training program regularly—like every second or third workout. And follow the tips for success listed here.

- Take three to five exercises that work well for each body part and use those as your pool of exercises to choose from for each workout.
- Choose two to three different exercises for each body part from the pool of exercises each workout.
- Do one basic movement (for example, incline dumbbell press) and one to two isolation movements (for example, dumbbell flyes, pec deck, or cable crossovers).
- Decrease your rest time between sets to no more than 60 seconds.
- Keep your reps in the 9 to 12 range for upper body and 12 to 25 range for legs.
- Each workout, vary the rest times, reps, sets, and weight. Keep your body constantly off-guard.
- Train abdominals at the beginning of your workout.
- Do no more than 8 sets per body part.
- Work out on a split training system. For example, on Monday work chest and arms, on Tuesday work legs, and on Wednesday work back and shoulders. Thursday is a day off from weight training, and you repeat the training schedule again on Friday.

THE ROLE OF THE BRAIN

One of the most important training tips for the endomorph to keep in mind is training intensity. The endomorph must constantly keep his training intensity high. Make the body work harder by working smarter, using the above guidelines. Keep the workouts fresh and exciting, and don't allow yourself to fall into a rut. Do something different each workout.

"We are not creatures of circumstance; we are creators of circumstance."

—Benjamin Disraeli

In life, rarely are you the victim of what happens to you; you're really the participant, the one who lets things happen to you. That is, until the day you decide that you're going to take charge of your life and not accept anything but the best you're capable of and that life has to give. Create your own circumstances by having unstoppable faith and belief in yourself, loving everyone, fearing nothing and no one, and taking focused action on every goal and dream inside your heart until you achieve it.

28

Training for the Mesomorph

Tips for the Easy Gainer

Blessed be the mesomorphs, those genetically gifted people who seem to gain muscle just by thinking about it. Well, not quite that easily, but mesomorphs are certainly bodybuilding's fastest muscle gainers. Yet despite their propensity to accumulate slabs of muscle in a hurry, mesomorphs need the right training and nutrition program to make the best gains possible.

MESOMORPH TRAINING NEEDS

The male mesomorph typically is muscular and naturally strong, with a long torso and a big, full chest. The female mesomorph is stronger and more muscular and often more athletic than other women. A mesomorph's strength can increase very quickly, as can her muscular size, especially on the right program.

A mesomorph responds well to training that involves heavy, quick movements, along with shaping exercises. The more varied the exercise program, the better the results. Take quads, for example. After a good warm-up, a mesomorph could begin with a great mass movement like squats, followed by hack squats or leg presses, finishing with a shaping movement like leg extensions.

For hamstrings, the mesomorph might begin with stiff-legged deadlifts, followed by a shaping movement such as standing leg curls. For calves, the first movement might be heavy standing calf raises followed by high-rep toe raises with light weight on the leg press.

THE MORE VARIABLES, THE BETTER

Mesomorphs should make repeated changes in the variables involved in working out—that is, the number of sets, reps, exercises, length of training sessions and rest, number of training days, amount of weight used, and various exercise angles. They should also vary their training intensity. A combination of three to four weeks of intense training followed by one to two weeks of lower-intensity training seems to promote growth and strength, and prevent training burnout.

THE MESOMORPH AND FOOD

Mesomorphs grow best when they get plenty of protein—at least 1 gram per pound of body weight daily—and keep their carb intake moderately high. The surprising thing about the majority of mesomorphs I know is that they can follow a diet with more than 20 percent of calories from fat (still far less than the typical American diet) and it actually helps them gain mass and strength!

In fact, many mesomorphs can boost their strength levels simply by increasing their fat and protein intake moderately. Strange as it may sound, a tablespoon or two of peanut butter a day can do some amazing things for a mesomorph.

A mesomorph typically will make strength and muscle gains by keeping his body weight relatively steady, looking to increase muscle mass only gradually. The days of bulking up by 20 or 30 pounds and then cutting down are over for the mesomorphs who want to gain the greatest amount of quality lean tissue. In fact, for all individuals, quality muscle size can be gained much more quickly when body fat levels are held under about 16 percent for men and about 22 percent for women.

THE AEROBIC FACTOR

If building muscle is the goal, intense cardiovascular work such as running should be kept to a minimum. Running long distances can be counterproductive—many mesomorphs can lose lean muscle tissue quickly if they run over two miles three times weekly. Some mesomorphs have found wind sprints an excellent way to condition and build the hamstrings, quads, and calves while aerobically conditioning the cardiovascular system.

If running isn't for you, try using the stairclimber, biking (stationary or road), racket sports, jumping rope, hiking, or walking (treadmill or regular). Just make sure you don't overdo it. Three times per week, 25 to 30 minutes per session (five-minute warm-up, 15 to 20 minutes in your target heart range, five-minute cool-down), will work well for burning fat.

Of course, you probably won't be able to do that when it comes to jumping rope. So jump for 3 to 12 minutes and rest only long enough to keep your heart rate in the target range. In fact, that's the key to doing all your cardiovascular exercise. To find your target heart range per minute, subtract your age from 220 and multiply by 0.6 and 0.8. That's where you should be exercising aerobically.

THE OVERMOTIVATION FACTOR

Since the mesomorph can make outstanding gains quickly, some individuals might be inclined to push themselves to the limit. Training intensely is great, but doing too much too quickly can lead to overtraining and injury.

Over the years, the sport of bodybuilding has been rife with genetically gifted mesomorphs with the potential for phenomenal growth and strength. But because of overenthusiasm, they either burned out, injured themselves, or lost motivation to continue training.

If you're a mesomorph, consider yourself fortunate. But be sensible with your training and nutrition—those two factors will help you reach your bodybuilding potential.

29

Training for the Ectomorph

When Putting on Size Is Hard to Do

In the last two chapters, we've discussed training for the endomorph and mesomorph body types. As you may recall, the endomorph gains size quickly but has to fight to keep the fat off. The mesomorph, bodybuilding's gifted body type, puts on lean muscle fairly easily and has an average to below-average body fat level.

That leaves the ectomorph, who tends to be thin, lean, and lanky. Typically, an ectomorph will have a short upper torso; long arms and legs; narrow chest, shoulders, feet and hands; and long, thin muscles.

Ectomorphs are leaders in the expedition for muscle size and weight. However hopeless it may seem for ectomorphs to gain slabs of beef or become champion bodybuilders, they shouldn't lose hope. Champions like three-time Mr. Olympia Frank Zane and many other great bodybuilders were at one time ectomorphs. Here are some training and nutrition tips that are sure to help the ectomorph in her muscle-building and strength-gaining goals.

USE POWER MOVEMENTS AND TRAIN HEAVY

The ectomorph needs to lift heavy weights to hit the deep muscle fibers that will make the body grow. Don't waste your time on isolation or cable movements right now. If you're an ectomorph, you should do the following:

Legs—squat, stiff-legged deadlift, donkey calf raise

Chest—dumbbell or barbell incline press

Back—chin-up; barbell, dumbbell, or T-bar row

Shoulders—dumbbell or barbell front press

Biceps—barbell or dumbbell curl

Triceps—close-grip bench press, dip, or lying EZ-bar French press

TAKE LONGER REST PERIODS

Ectomorphs tend to train at a fast pace, and would benefit greatly—both in recovery and strength—if they slowed down. Intense training is the stimulus that creates muscle growth. Intensity can be accomplished in a number of ways; two of the best are heavy lifting and longer rest between sets, and lighter lifting with shorter rest time.

Because high-intensity workouts are necessary to make the ectomorph grow, their focus should be on lifting heavier and taking longer rest periods between sets to ensure greater muscular recovery for maximum intensity and strength for each set.

Ectomorphs must also give their bodies adequate rest between workouts. The absolute *minimum* rest an ectomorph needs is 48 hours between the same body part workouts. And they should never work a body part unless it has *fully* recovered from the previous workout. Because of their high metabolism, ectomorphs should get no less than seven and a half hours (preferably eight to nine) of sleep every night.

THE NUTRITION FACTOR

Training is unquestionably an important element in the ectomorph's bodybuilding success, but good nutrition is too! In fact, one of the biggest reasons ectomorphs have so many problems is that they eat too many of the wrong foods and too little of the good foods, and don't eat often enough. Let's simplify things. You should structure your diet in the following way.

- Eat five to seven small meals daily.
- Increase your daily protein intake to 1 to 1.5 grams of protein per pound of body weight.
- Aim to get protein intake to no less than 35 percent of your daily total caloric intake.
- Have a protein shake 90 minutes before bedtime.

- Carbs should be 45 percent of daily dietary intake.
- Increase your daily intake of fibrous carbs (cauliflower, broccoli) while limiting your intake of simple sugars (fruit, honey).
- Keep your fat intake to roughly 20 percent of your daily dietary intake.
- Eat slower-burning glycemic-index foods such as beans, sweet corn, lentils, yams, peas, nonfat dairy products, porridge, oats, and pasta. (The *glycemic index* ranks food on a scale of 1 to 100 according to how quickly its carbohydrates increase glucose, or blood sugar, levels in comparison to glucose itself. The lower the glycemic number, the slower the increase; the higher the number, the faster the increase.)
- Supplement with a good multivitamin/mineral.
- Drink lots of water throughout the day—at least 80 ounces.

KEEP STRESS LEVELS LOW

Many ectomorphs are high-strung individuals. They're usually amped up and on the go. For such individuals, stress can be a problem—it affects progress in the gym by producing cortisol, a catabolic (tissue-destroying) hormone.

Ectomorphs should practice slowing things down and relaxing. Try slowing your pace, and take at least 10 minutes a day to be alone and away from people and noise. In those 10 minutes, lie down or sit relaxed, close your eyes, inhale through your mouth and exhale through your nose, and slowly and softly repeat the words "calm," "serenity," and "tranquil." Feel your muscles relax and become heavy, as if concrete weights were attached to them. Imagine that all stress is leaving your body and dissipating in the air. Nothing can bother you. You are in control.

MINIMIZE OUTSIDE ACTIVITIES

Because most ectomorphs have metabolisms as fast as a greyhound's, their bodies tend to burn the food they eat very quickly. Many ectomorphs I've talked to complain that they can't put on size. For good reason: they don't eat enough of the right foods, they don't train correctly, and they engage in too much activity.

If you're an ectomorph and your big goal is to pack on more size and strength, minimize all other activities outside of weight training. Your goal is to make sure your body uses all the nutrients you consume in order to recover and grow from your bodybuilding workouts.

If you must be involved in other physically demanding activities, be sure to take in extra calories—above those you are taking in for bodybuilding—and get plenty of rest. Follow these guidelines, and your weight- and strength-gaining problems will be history.

"The great man is he who does not lose his child's heart."

–Mencius

It's time for you to be a kid again. Of course, working out makes you feel young and strong, and the great thing is that those feelings will stay with you for the rest of your life—all for the price of a workout! But don't let it stop there. Stop being so serious about things, especially life! As one great thinker put it, "Life is much too important to be taken seriously." How true, how true. For heaven's sake, start enjoying yourself and start really having a good time every day of your life by being the kid inside you who never wanted to grow up when the rest of you did.

PART V

Best Exercises and Ways to Make Them Even Better

30

Building a Great Routine: The Best Exercises for Quads

The ideal routine. Wouldn't we all love to have it? If your routine isn't all that you hoped it would be, don't be discouraged. Every bodybuilder—from the champion to the rank beginner—is constantly searching for that magical exercise that will make her muscles grow as they never have before. After all, the quest for physical perfection is neverending.

In this chapter, we'll talk about great exercises, starting with quads. Before we begin, here are a few key points to remember about quad training:

1. Before beginning any heavy leg work, always be sure to warm up, and use strict exercise form to help avoid injury.
2. Use heavy weights with 6 to 10 reps for building quad mass.
3. Quads also respond very well to high reps. Some bodybuilders think 15 to 20 reps is high. However, I know many great bodybuilders who'll do 50 to 75 reps per set on leg presses and leg extensions to shock their quads into growth.
4. Make the muscle burn. In other words, if you aren't feeling the pump, the exercise won't do jack squat for you. Forget trying to impress people who couldn't care less about how much you can lift.

With all that in mind, here are some of the finest quad exercises you can do.

SQUATS

The majority of champions whose legs are huge got them that way by one exercise—the squat! Champions will tell you the squat is the king of all leg exercises. Sure, a good squat workout will zap you. However, you won't reach your full bodybuilding potential without it. Not only that, the squat is an exercise that stimulates metabolic rate and leg and peripheral muscle growth. In other words, you simply can't beat the squat. Here are the variations.

Front Squat
Arguably the best of all squats. Sure, you can't go nearly as heavy as you

could with the back squat (some estimate 30 to 50 percent less weight), but you'll get far better results. Front squats will work the quad more intensely, give it greater sweep, force you to employ strict form, and prevent you from using your back to bend over and cheat.

Back Squat

The difference between this and the front squat is that the bar rests on your traps or upper back and not across the clavicles and front delts. Lots of weight can be squatted using this popular version. However, be sure to use strict form, and keep your back and neck in the straight-up position throughout the movement. For best results, go down until your quads are parallel to the floor.

Smith Machine Squat

Both front and back squats can be done on this machine. Many bodybuilders like the Smith machine because the bar travels along guide rods in a fixed up-and-down position, thus making balance much less of a problem.

Sissy Squat

This is actually a nonweighted squat. That's right, you use just your body weight. However, do 30 sissy squats after your regular weighted quad workout, and you'll know why people who do them aren't sissies. Get ready for a major burn!

Machine Hack Squat

Hacks are usually performed on an angled sled-type machine. The foot platform can be elevated to varying degrees to hit different areas of the quad. The steeper the angle, the greater the emphasis on the lower muscles.

Barbell Hack Squat

A great variation of the machine hack squat is performed with a moderately weighted barbell. Stand with a wooden block or two barbell plates under your heels. Hold the barbell behind you, keeping it placed firmly against the hamstrings and glutes. With the upper body erect, bend your legs and squat down until your quads are nearly parallel to the floor. Go for reps of 10 to 15.

OTHER GREAT QUAD EXERCISES

Leg Press

An excellent mass builder. Not only can you use heavy weight, but your back, glutes, and upper torso are supported, allowing you to concentrate on working your quads. You'll find that the leg press comes in a few different variations; the two most common are the 45- and 90-degree leg press.

Leg Extension

Undoubtedly one of the best quad shapers and separators around. High reps of 12 to 25 work very well on this exercise. Pointing your feet straight will work the overall quads. Feet turned outward will hit the inner quad. Feet turned inward will hit the outer quad. Use either a flat seat to hit the overall quads, or a decline-angle seat to hit the upper quad.

Lunge

Arnold Schwarzenegger once thought this exercise was worthless—that is, until he saw the incredible separation it gave his quads. You can experience similar results. As with any exercise, strict form is necessary to get the most from lunges. You don't need heavy weights for this movement. Making the muscle burn with reps of 15 to 30 will get the best results. For variety, do one lunge workout with a barbell and the next with dumbbells.

31

Building a Great Chest

Design Your Routine Around These Exercises

Big, thick pecs. Size in this body part—besides gigantic arms—is undoubtedly the most sought-after among beginners. The key to building a big chest for both novices and champions alike is simple: proper training.

A bigger chest is near the top of most bodybuilders' wish list. So why don't more lifters—those who work out six days a week and those who barely work out twice a week—have the chest they want? Is it the wrong routine? Lack of training intensity? Weights too light? It could be all of these. However, not knowing the best exercises ranks at the top.

In the last chapter, we talked about great quad exercises. Now let's talk chest—I mean *big* chest! These exercises have passed the acid test for producing consistent and solid results. And although I could devote pages to the how-tos of these exercises, for now just use the following information as a guide. Experiment with the exercises. Put them together in new combinations and find which work best for you.

Remember: the key to bodybuilding success is the right mix of exercises with maximum training intensity, proper nutrients and supplements, and sufficient rest and recuperation. With that in mind, here are some of the best chest exercises.

Incline Barbell Press

The bench press, according to some folks, is *the* exercise for building mass and chest power. But I disagree—I think the incline barbell press is better. I've seen scores of bodybuilders who concentrate on doing flat bench press movements. And while their middle and lower chest and front delts are well-developed, their upper-chest thickness lags way behind. Conversely, I've seen bodybuilders whose main pectoral movement is incline presses, and their *entire* chests—from top to bottom—are full and complete.

Real-world advice: concentrate on upper-chest work, and the rest of your chest development will fall into place. The exercise is a good choice for learning the mechanics of incline pressing and establishing an exercise groove. Always bring the elbows down and back, and make the bar touch the top of your upper pecs, just below the neck.

Incline Dumbbell Press

My number-one preference for all chest work. Dumbbells allow you to get a fuller range of motion by giving you a deeper stretch. Also, the groove isn't as rigidly fixed as it is when using a barbell or machine. Using dumbbells requires the stabilizer muscles (delts, triceps) to work harder, thus working those muscle groups too.

Smith Machine Incline Press

Many bodybuilders like the Smith machine because the bar travels in a groove. I recommend using it only occasionally to provide variety to your workout. Your upper-chest training should concentrate on the basics: barbells and dumbbells.

Bench Press

This exercise has long been the yardstick by which most bodybuilders measure strength. As early as high school, I can remember people asking, *How much can you bench?* Few people care about how heavy you lift in movements like, say, a bent-over lateral.

Most bodybuilders get the best results by doing the following:

- Keep your feet on the ground and your glutes, upper back, and shoulders firmly on the bench, with only a slight arch in the back.
- Keep your arms close to your body at the bottom of the movement.
- Exhale forcefully as you press the barbell up, and inhale as you lower the weight.

Dumbbell Press

This is a version of the bench press that many bodybuilders prefer over the one with the barbell. Dumbbells allow a deeper stretch, greater contraction, and more fiber recruitment, all of which mean greater results.

Smith Machine Bench Press

The groove in which the bar travels makes this a great way to work the entire chest, depending on elbow position and where the bar touches the chest. Try this flat bench variation for upper chest. The farther you bring the upper arms toward the head (the elbows move back into a straight line across the body), the greater the pec stretch. Lower the bar until it touches the upper chest. Keep the bar moving steadily and the weights light (since the shoulder is in a somewhat compromised position) until you get a feel for the movement.

Decline Barbell Press

This is an excellent exercise for hitting the lower chest. Many bodybuilders bring the bar down to lower-chest level, but if you want better results, reduce the weight and bring the elbows up and back and let the bar touch near the top of the upper chest. A few inches can make a huge difference!

Decline Dumbbell Press

You'll probably need a partner or spotter to help get the dumbbells into the starting position. Use only a moderate weight until you get a feel for the dumbbells.

Smith Machine Decline Press

The execution of this movement is the same as that of the decline barbell press, except you don't have to concentrate on balancing the weight throughout the movement, as the bar travels along a fixed path. Smith machines are a great way to find the right groove because they allow you to experiment to find which bar-to-body position is best for you.

ASSISTANCE MOVEMENTS

While more famous for being shaping movements (with the exception of dips and the vertical pec press), one of the following assistance movements should be included in every chest workout.

Dumbbell Flye

This is one of the best shaping movements. Try using different bench angles (incline, flat, decline), and keep the elbows bent slightly and the arms wide. Don't let the dumbbells touch each other at the top.

Cable Crossovers

Lots of pros use this exercise (especially before a contest) to bring out more chest definition. For added intensity, bend over at the waist so that the upper body is almost parallel to the floor during the entire movement.

Pec Deck Machine

This machine is a real chest burner. Place your feet on a bench or seat in front of you to keep your back braced firmly against the vertical back pad. The farther you place your arms in front of and away from your body, the harder you work the chest.

Dip

Often thought of as a chest-finishing movement, dips are also one of the best lower-pec mass builders around. Once you're able to do 2 or 3 sets of 12 to 15 reps, use a weight belt with a chain or strap and do weighted dips with a plate or dumbbell.

Vertical Pec Press

This seated exercise is similar in effect to a machine bench press where you're lying down. Keep your feet firmly on the ground to help keep your upper torso braced against the vertical back pad. Most machines give you an option in hand placement, so try varying your hand position: keep hands close together to hit the inner chest, and keep hands spread apart to hit the outer chest.

"As soon as you trust yourself, you will know how to live."

—Johann Wolfgang von Goethe

My friend, the only way you will ever know how something is, is to experience it. You can talk to 10 people about the same thing, and they'll give you 10 different answers. Yet none of them is right—because for you, the only right answer is the answer you and you alone get when you experience something. Don't be afraid to try new workouts, routines, exercises, foods, or anything else. Only you will know if they are right for you. Trust yourself.

32

Trick Moves for Arms and Abs

Mass-Exercise Variations

Allow me to take a page out of Mike Mentzer's seminar book. Mike often starts his seminars by asking the audience, *Has anybody grown too fast lately—grown so fast that it's bothered you?* Of course, nobody ever raises a hand. Well, don't despair. I'm going to give you some exercise variations for mass-building that will do wonders for your biceps, triceps, and abs.

Keep this in mind before you get started: heavy weights are only secondary to strict form. You must feel the movement. Too much weight prevents you from really feeling the muscle burn. If you don't feel it, reduce the weight until you can feel a maximal contraction in every rep.

BICEPS

I'm giving you three biceps movements that will dramatically improve your biceps peak. When doing these, remember to keep your upper arms and elbows stationary; move only the hands and forearms.

Supported Bench Barbell Curl

Most bodybuilders do supported T-bar rows on this bench. You, however, can do a very effective barbell or EZ-bar curl. Position yourself so that your chest and

Supported bench barbell curl (a)

Supported bench barbell curl (b)

head are above the upper portion of the pad. Have a partner hand you a barbell, and take a moderately wide grip.

With elbows slightly forward and turned in, curl the barbell up to shoulder level (or the point where you feel the greatest biceps contraction). Squeeze the biceps for one to two seconds, and slowly lower the bar until your arms are fully extended. Do 12 to 20 reps.

Lying Dumbbell Curl

With two light dumbbells, lie down on a flat bench. Lower your arms down and out to your sides. Position your elbows close to the bench, but turn your hands out and away. Without moving your elbows, curl the dumbbells up and supinate your wrists (turn the hands out by bringing the little finger higher than the thumb) once you reach the top position. Squeeze your

Lying dumbbell curl (a)

Lying dumbbell curl (b)

biceps in this position for one to two seconds, then slowly lower the weights, keeping the elbows stationary. Fully extend your arms and repeat. Go to failure.

Squat-Position Barbell Curl

This is a great finishing movement for biceps. Reps is the key word here—lots of them! Take a close grip on a light barbell or EZ-bar. Squat down and place your arms against the inside of your thighs. Keep your upper torso erect. Curl the barbell up to chin level,

Squat-position barbell curl (a)

Squat-position barbell curl (b)

and hold the peak contraction for a count. Slowly lower the weight until the arms are again fully extended. Do 15 to 25 reps.

TRICEPS

For biceps, we concentrated on peak. For triceps, we're working on mass. Keep in mind that in triceps exercises, the position of your elbow and upper arm is extremely important. Generally, the closer you keep them to your head or upper body, the harder your triceps work. Always remember to contract your triceps hard with your arms fully extended, and stretch them as you lower the weight.

Kneeling Cable French Press

This exercise is excellent for hitting the long head of the triceps. Be sure to keep your upper arms close to your head from start to finish. Kneel down with your back to the weight stack. Grab a curved bar or rope connected to a low pulley. Bring your hands behind you as you position your upper arms close to your head. Raise the bar or rope just above your head until your arms are fully extended and elbows locked. Hold it with the arms in the fully extended position for one to two seconds. Slowly lower the weight as far as possible for a deep stretch. Do 12 to 20 reps.

Bench Dip

If your triceps are lacking size just above the elbow, then this is the exercise for you. Place two flat benches side by side about three feet apart. With your heels resting on one bench, hold onto the edge of the other with your palms facing behind you. Lock your arms to support your body weight. Keep your back three to six inches away from the side of the bench throughout the entire movement.

Kneeling cable French press (a)

Kneeling cable French press (b)

Bench dip (a)

Bench dip (b)

With your upper arms and elbows pointed straight back, have a partner place a barbell plate on top of your thighs for extra resistance. If you can't use a plate yet, that's okay. You will soon. Lower your body as far as possible, and push back up. Go to nearly full extension—this helps keep the stress on the lower triceps. Do 20 to 30 reps.

Close-Grip Bench Press

This exercise is a major triceps mass packer. Position yourself on a flat bench as if you were doing a bench press. Keep your legs elevated and crossed, and grip the bar with your hands spaced about 6 to 10 inches apart. With arms close to your upper torso, lower the bar under control to lower chest level. Push the bar back up and lock the elbows to get full triceps contraction. Do 6 to 10 reps.

ABS

This is such a beautiful muscle group, and it's the centerpiece of a great physique. You've got to make the abs burn to get the best results. You don't need a long range of motion when training abs. That's right—short, concentrated, nonstop reps work best.

Roman Chair Sit-Up

At one time, this was *the* exercise for serious bodybuilders—chances were you'd find someone on the Roman chair at any serious gym. Then Nautilus machines and the like came on the scene, and the Roman chair became something of a dinosaur. What do you say we resurrect the dinosaur for Jurassic ab results?

If your gym has a Roman chair, use it. If one is unavailable, simply sit on the side of a flat bench. Place your feet flat on the floor and underneath an immovable object. Your upper legs should be parallel to the floor.

Take a plate and hold it firmly against your chest. Lean back at a 30- to 45-degree angle, and then squeeze and contract your abs by coming up until your upper torso is nearly vertical. Be sure to breathe in as you lean back and exhale as you come forward. Keep the reps going, and don't stop until you've done 20 to 30.

Close-grip bench press (a)

Close-grip bench press (b)

Crunch (a)

Crunch (b)

Crunch

Lots of bodybuilders do crunches with their calves resting on top of a flat bench. Nothing wrong with that. So when someone told me I would feel crunches more intensely if my lower legs were immobilized—as in someone sitting on them—I said "Prove it." He did! My body no longer moved that extra inch or two—a distance significant enough to reduce the intensity of the exercise—as I crunched. Holding my legs down prevented this.

Simply position yourself as if you're doing a regular crunch. Keep your thighs vertical (bring your glutes close to the bench) and your calves resting on top of the bench. While a partner holds your feet down, curl your upper torso up for a full contraction. Hold it for one to two seconds, then slowly lower your upper body only a few inches, and repeat. Keep constant tension in your abs in this limited range of motion. Go for 30 reps.

Side Crunch

This exercise will put an end to your excuses for poor serratus muscles. Do this movement on the back extension bench, lying on the side of your hips. Place your legs, one on top of the other, under the ankle pad. Raise your upper torso sideways to contract your serratus as strongly as possible. Lower yourself to a level in line with your legs. Do 20 to 30 reps per side.

Side crunch (a)

Side crunch (b)

33

Tricks for Quads, Hamstrings, and Calves

If you're like most bodybuilders, you've found that basic exercises are great. But what if you want to do something different? Maybe something a little out of the ordinary. Are you limited to just the basics? Absolutely not!

In this chapter, we'll deal with more variations for building mass—great ones for quads, hamstrings, and calves. Not only that, I'm going to give you growth-enhancing training techniques—the Weider principles—that will help you pack on some serious size and strength. First, let's look at quads.

Sissy Squat

Not many people do these. Too bad—they're a fantastic quad builder. To get the most from them, use strict form, high reps, and minimal rest (no more than 45 seconds rest between sets).

Keep your feet and knees close together throughout the entire movement. Hold onto a machine, bench, or vertical bar for support, but hold on only for balance, and not to help you cheat. While keeping your body straight, leaning back at a 30- to 70-degree angle, lower your body over

your feet and come back up to near lockout. Go for as many reps as possible. Don't stop when the quads start burning—really feel them pump.

FOR ADDED MUSCLE BURN: Try compound-setting leg extensions (15 reps) to sissy squats (limit).

Hack Squat (Barbell Under Glutes)

The hack squat is a terrific way to develop the inner vastus (the teardrop-shaped muscle above your knee) and outer-thigh sweep. You've probably used the hack squat machine, so you should have a pretty good idea of the mechanics. However, you can make things a bit more intense by holding a barbell under your glutes.

Place your heels on a block of wood or two barbell plates. With a slightly wider than shoulder-width overhand grip, hold a barbell under your glutes. With your feet about 12 inches apart, keeping your upper torso upright, squat down until your thighs are parallel with the floor. When returning to the starting position, stop

Sissy squat (a)

Sissy squat (b)

Hack squat (a)

Hack squat (b)

about three-quarters of the way. This helps to keep constant tension in your quads. Go for 12 to 20 nonstop reps.

FOR ADDED MUSCLE BURN: Try using partial reps once you've reached full-rep failure.

Leg Extension (Lying on Back)

For a major burn in the upper quads, this is the exercise. The movement is the same as the seated leg extension; the only difference is that you lie flat on the horizontal support pad from start to finish. Go for 15 to 25 reps.

FOR ADDED MUSCLE BURN: Try using descending sets. After you've completed 10 reps with a heavy weight, immediately reduce the weight by 30 percent and do 5 to 10 more reps. Then immediately reduce the weight once more by 30 percent and crank out another 5 to 10 reps.

HAMSTRINGS

When it comes to building a muscle, many bodybuilders will just go through the motions if they can't see the muscle work. Take the hamstrings. Sure, they're easy to see in the mirror when you're standing sideways. But try watching them work when you're doing a set of leg curls! If you can't see the muscle, your mental focus can be greatly diminished.

With that in mind, try to focus more on the hamstrings when you work them. When doing leg curls, reduce the poundage you are now using; go for the reps, and really feel the muscles contract and stretch.

Stiff-Legged Deadlift (Dumbbells)

This is pretty much the same movement as the barbell stiff-legged deadlift, except here you use dumbbells. The

Stiff-legged deadlift (a)

Stiff-legged deadlift (b)

other difference is that the dumbbells will come down to the outside of your calves, not in front of your shins. This will help reduce unnecessary lower-back and shoulder stress.

Keep your back slightly arched throughout the exercise. Try not to let your back round as you lower the dumbbells. Rounding the back may allow you to get a few more inches of stretch, but you won't feel the movement as much in your hamstrings.

FOR ADDED MUSCLE BURN: Try using tri-sets. Do a set of lying leg curls (to fail-

ure) immediately followed by a set of standing leg curls (to failure), then do dumbbell stiff-legged deadlifts (6 to 9 reps) as your final movement.

CALVES

The calf muscles are tricky to develop. You use them in walking, so you do hundreds of thousands of reps every day with your body weight. But since walking (low intensity) works the calves in less than an optimum form for growth, here are a few ways to make them work harder and grow.

Smith Machine Standing Calf Raise (Front and Back)

This looks like a regular standing calf raise, but it doesn't feel like one! You're going to need a Smith machine and a small platform to elevate your feet so you can get a good heel stretch.

Now, do these two ways: bar across your back (like a back squat) and bar across the front delts (like a front squat). Keep only the balls of your feet on the edge of the platform for optimum stretch. Keep your body straight and in the upright position throughout the movement. Move only your ankles.

In the first set, place the platform directly under the bar so that your body and feet are in a straight line. Next set, move the platform slightly forward. On the third set, move the platform slightly backward. You will feel the difference! Do at least 25 reps per set.

FOR ADDED MUSCLE BURN: Try using forced reps. Once you reach the point of full-rep failure, have a partner grab the bar and push up with just enough help to allow you to do a few more full-range reps. Use forced reps sparingly.

Calf Slide Machine

Talk about a machine with a great angle to stretch the calves! Let me suggest a cool way to do these that will work the inner calf. With your feet pointed straight ahead and shoulder-width apart, bring your quads together. Your leg and foot position will resemble a Y.

Concentrate all the weight of the movement on the inside of the balls of the feet, especially over the big toes. Lower the heels as far as possible, and then back up as high as you can. Go for at least 20 reps, resting no longer than 35 seconds between sets.

FOR ADDED MUSCLE BURN: Pyramid your weights. Start out with light weight. Do at least 20 reps for warm-up, then go up 50 percent in weight each succeeding set.

Smith machine standing calf raise (a)

Smith machine standing calf raise (b)

> **"Know the three big lies: What I don't have is better than what
> I've got. More is always better. I'll be happy when I finally get what
> I want."**
>
> You want to know the truth? You're not going to be happy even when you reach your ideal fitness and body-building goals. And you know, that's okay—and here's why. You're human: and as a human, you're basically a goal-seeking and goal-achieving being. As soon as you achieve one goal, you're ready for the next one. And that's the way it should be. That's how you grow, learn, and develop into the person you were meant to be. So when you have those days when you think you'll be happy once you reach your goal, or that if you could get what you want that'd make all the difference in the world, just remember that it won't and it was never meant to. Keep dreaming those dreams and achieving them, and you'll be so happy doing what you love that you won't even think about all those other lies.

34

Tricks for Growing a Bigger Chest, Back, and Shoulders

Earlier in the book, we talked about the basic building blocks of knowledge for the beginner, intermediate, and advanced bodybuilder. Now it's time to get into those exercises that are great for building slabs of muscle on the chest, back, and shoulders, many of which you have probably seen or used. Others may be new. But we're not stopping there. You also need to know about certain exercise variations that will allow you to get even more out of each exercise.

CHEST

Along with weighted dips, presses (incline, flat, and decline) are tremendous mass packers for the chest. However, not all presses are created equal. For example, flat benches primarily hit the middle chest, incline presses work the upper chest, and declines focus on the lower pecs. Yet by simply changing bar and elbow positions, you can take a movement for middle chest and turn it into a terrific upper-chest developer. Here's how.

Bench Press (For Upper Chest)
The ideal way to perform this is with a Smith machine, since the bar travels up and down along a guide rod in a fixed position. If a Smith machine is not available, use a barbell and regular flat bench.

Bench press

Decline barbell press

With hands slightly wider than shoulder-width, bring the bar down to just below the neck. At the bottom position, make sure your elbows are back toward your head. Complete 10 to 15 reps.

Decline Barbell Press (For Lower Chest)

Declines are a great low-pec developer. The trouble is that most bodybuilders do them incorrectly by lowering the bar only to the lower chest and not to the top of the upper chest. (When doing this exercise, make sure you have a spotter, or do them on the Smith machine.)

To do the exercise correctly, take a grip on the bar slightly wider than shoulder-width. Simultaneously bring your elbows downward and back as you lower the bar to upper-chest/lower-neck level. Make sure the bar touches the very top of your upper chest.

You'll have to reduce the weight you usually lift on this exercise—probably by 50 percent! That's okay, because now you'll be doing the movement correctly for maximal fiber stretch and activation, which translates into greater results. Do 6 to 10 reps.

Straight-Arm Pec Deck

Lots of bodybuilders love the pec deck as a finishing movement to their chest routines. And it can be a great movement—if you do it right. Unfortunately,

Straight-arm pec deck

BACK

The back is made up of so many muscles that it takes several exercises to train all of them completely. But doing lots of exercises isn't enough. When doing rows and pulldowns, you must slightly arch the back and bring the elbows straight back behind you to get a maximal contraction. Forget using heavy weights until you can make each rep a maximally contracted rep! Sample these exercises to add slabs of back muscle.

Reverse-Grip Row (With Ez-Bar)

Barbell rows have been around for years. However, it wasn't until recently that reverse-grip barbell rows became the back builder of choice for many bodybuilders. And for good reason: they work! In fact, many bodybuilders who do them correctly say that the exercise hits the outer lats from top to bottom.

Do them with a shoulder-width reverse grip. With legs slightly bent and upper torso at a 50- to 70-degree angle, bring your elbows directly back behind you and pull the barbell into your waist.

That's exactly how you should do them with a barbell, but I want you to try them with an EZ-bar. The EZ-bar will take the stress off the wrists and biceps. You'll find that the exercise is easier to do, and that your ability to concentrate on the movement (and keep the back slightly arched for maximal contraction) will increase. Go for 5 to 9 reps.

Close-Grip T-Bar Row

T-bar rows can be done with a variety of grips: wide, to hit the middle back; and medium, to hit mid to outer lats. But if you really want to hit the outer lats—even the tie-ins next to the intercostals—then take a very close grip!

On the center of the bar, below where the T handle is connected, grip

many are lessening the effectiveness of the movement when they move their upper torsos away from the vertical back pad and bend forward to squeeze the pads together.

Try it this way. Keep your back firmly against the vertical backrest. With the pads resting against the insides of your arms, fully extend each arm (which will be out to your sides when you begin the exercise) and keep them fully extended throughout the exercise. At the top of the movement (when the pads are directly in front of you), be sure to touch the pads together and hold the contraction for a count or two. No set rep range is used on this—do as many reps as possible.

Reverse-grip row

Close-grip T-bar row

the bar with the left hand in front of the right. With legs slightly bent, bend over until your upper torso is about parallel with the floor.

Pull the bar up until the plates touch your chest. Lower the bar completely; your arms should be fully extended at this point. Let the shoulders relax, and you should gain another two inches of lat stretch. Alternate hand positions on each set. Do 6 to 9 reps.

Behind-Neck Pulldown (Stirrup Bar)

Pulldowns are an excellent alternative to pullups for those who aren't yet able to do 8 or more reps per set. And one of the best middle- and upper-back developers happens to be the behind-neck pulldown.

Let's go one step further and really make those middle- and upper-back muscles work by using a stirrup bar, a neutral grip (palms facing each other), and slow, strict reps. Bring the bar down and touch the traps—really squeeze the back muscles as you bring the bar down. Do 8 to 12 reps.

Behind-neck pulldown

SHOULDERS AND TRAPS

In reality, shoulders are such a small muscle group that it's easy to overtrain them. Shoulders respond well to heavy weights—as well as light weights and high reps—but not too heavy and not too often.

The shoulder joint is vulnerable, and doing behind-neck barbell presses with too much weight and a too-wide grip can lead to injury. These nonpressing movements are guaranteed to make your delts and traps pump and grow.

Rear Delt Lateral Cable Raise
Probably the best known way to work rear delts is with bent-over dumbbell laterals. Another way to really smoke 'em is with cables. Place a flat bench about three feet away from a low pulley. With one hand, grab a stirrup handle and lie down on your side facing the low-cable pulley.

Bring the arm up and back in line with the body. Squeeze the rear delt at the top peak-contracted position, then slowly lower the cable back down and repeat. Go for reps of 12 to 20 for each side.

Behind-Body Cable Side Lateral
In Arnold Schwarzenegger's *The Encyclopedia of Bodybuilding*, Arnold is pictured doing this exercise. Talk about showing his incredibly separated delts.

Rear delt lateral cable raise

What inspiration! And if you do them correctly, you're bound to be inspired by the results that will soon be apparent.

Place a small bench about three feet away from and directly in front of a low pulley. With the cable handle in your left hand, sit on the end of the bench with your right side next to the apparatus. With the cable behind your body, raise your left arm out to your side and up to shoulder level. Hold in the peak contracted position for a count, then slowly lower and repeat. Go for 12 to 20 reps for each side.

Standing Calf Machine Shrug

And you thought the standing calf machine was just for calves. It's a great way to work your traps, and you don't even have to hold onto anything. With feet flat on the floor or on the block, position yourself under the standing calf machine, just like you would if you were going to do standing calf raises.

With the pads resting on your shoulders, legs straight and upper torso erect, lower your shoulders, then shrug them up as high as possible. Hold the

Behind-body cable
side lateral

Standing calf machine shrug

shoulders up and keep the traps in the fully contracted position for one to two seconds, then slowly lower the shoulders and repeat. Do as many reps as possible.

Just remember that the exercise variations described in this chapter are just that—variations. That means they are subject to change based on your body type and how you best feel each movement.

Bodybuilding is a thinking person's sport. So regardless of whether you're a beginner, intermediate, or advanced bodybuilder, the more you think about how you can make each exercise and all its variations work for you, the faster you'll grow and the stronger you'll get.

35

The Nuances for Results

Why do people spend money on gym memberships and equipment, when they exercise incorrectly and get little, if any, results? Good question—and I have no answer. The truth is, *very few* people work out with *maximum* effectiveness.

I believe that learning how to feel an exercise—I mean really getting into each rep and making those reps pump the muscle and make it burn—is the key. Whether you're short or tall, fat or thin, young or old, if you can feel an exercise, it's going to work!

Did you ever notice how differently you feel an exercise just by changing the position of your hands, feet, or elbows? If you haven't experimented with this, it's time you did! Slight variations or nuances force your body to use different muscle fibers and neural pathways, working your muscles at different angles and thereby giving you better results.

Let's look at some simple exercise nuances you can use right now that can make a huge difference in your training. *Remember, form is everything.*

THE FOOT NUANCE

You've got to have a lot of sole to do this! You can change foot position three ways to hit the calf and thigh muscles differently. In the standing calf raise, pointing your feet straight will work the overall calf. I've found that turning my feet outward seems to hit my inner calves more, while turning them inward hits my outer calves. Try it and see if it works for you, too.

Let's move to the hack squat machine. To minimize stress on the knees, place your feet high up on the foot platform. Keep your heels together and turn your feet outward. You've now directed the emphasis to the inner thigh. By keeping your feet and legs together and pointed straight, you'll direct the emphasis to the outer thigh—an excellent way to develop a fabulous quad sweep.

As you probably know, the squat is one of the best leg exercises. Yet some beginners and intermediates may find some of the squat variations difficult. One such variation involves

placing the legs almost in a direct line with the upper torso, feet wider than shoulder-width and turned outward. *The knees must travel in a direct line over the middle toes.* Obviously, the weight used in this exercise must be fairly light to minimize injury and maintain ideal form.

One way to do this exercise correctly is with a Smith machine. Because the bar travels in a fixed position, you can experiment to find the optimal leg position without having to worry about stabilizing the upper body. Many call this a ballet squat. For hitting the inner thigh, upper-outer thigh, and glutes, this exercise is a killer! Go for 12 to 20 reps.

THE NUANCE OF ANGLE

Do a barbell curl on a steep-sided (90-degree) preacher bench, and you'll feel the stress in the upper biceps. Do that same curl on the opposite side of the bench (at a 45-degree angle), and you'll feel it in the lower biceps.

Legs are a terrific body part for exercises using different angles. Do a 30-degree leg press, and you'll feel it in your lower quads; do one at 45 degrees or higher, and you'll feel the pressure in the upper quads and hamstrings.

Lower the foot platform on the hack squat, and you'll feel the stress in your upper quads. Raise the platform, and the emphasis shifts to the lower quad area just above the knee. And don't forget leg extensions. The knees-angled-down position works the lower quads and inner vastus. The knees-angled-up position works the upper quads.

THE ELBOW NUANCE

Just moving your elbow up or down, into the body or away, can also make a big difference. Most bodybuilders do the triceps dumbbell kickback with their upper arm in line with their upper torso. But to really make the triceps scream, keep the upper arm close to the body and raise the upper arm and elbow up and above the upper torso. The higher you raise it, the harder it

gets. Be sure to lock the arm out at the top of the movement.

Another great triceps exercise is the pressdown. Here's a trick you can use to feel the same exercise, with the same hand grip, in different parts of the triceps, simply by moving your elbows. Take a fairly close grip (six to eight inches apart) on a straight bar. With elbows close to your body, do a set of 10 to 12 reps of pressdowns. Now, keeping the same grip, move your elbows out and away from your body, almost in a direct line with your upper torso. Be sure to lock your arms out at the bottom of the movement. Where do you feel each movement? So simple, yet so effective.

And let's not forget the seated dumbbell curl. Elbows in, elbows out, elbows back, or elbows forward hits the same biceps in many different ways. Experiment and find which ones make your biceps beg for mercy the most!

THE HAND NUANCE

Simply by moving your hands, you can feel the same exercise in many different ways. Take, for example, the barbell curl. After you've taken a wide grip, place your elbows close to your body. As you curl the weight up, you should feel the stress on the outer biceps. Lower the bar and move your hands close together (four to six inches apart). Now the stress is placed on the inner biceps.

Try the seated cable row for the back. Many bodybuilders use a stirrup bar that places the hands close together; try using a straight pulldown bar. On one set, keep your hands spaced wide. If you keep your elbows out away from your body, you should feel the movement more toward the center of your back. For the next set, bring your hands close together (six to eight inches apart) and pull with your

elbows in close to your sides. You should now feel it in the outer lats.

And don't forget the old tried-and-true method of hand pronation—turning the palms down—when doing triceps pressdowns. Use a rope instead of a bar. Keep your elbows close to your sides. At the bottom of the movement, pronate your hands and lock your arms out and hold the peak con-

traction for one to two seconds. Really feel the triceps burn. Just those few inches of hand pronation can make a big difference!

THE NUANCE OF GRIP

Take a wide grip on a barbell and do an incline press. Where do you feel it?

Outer chest. Move your hands closer together, and you'll feel it more in the inner chest and triceps. Same exercise, yet two very different ways of hitting the same muscle.

Use a wide grip on chin-ups, and you'll feel more upper lat and teres; a closer grip with the elbows moving downward from the front of the body hits more lower lat. Experiment with various positions on every grip-involved exercise you do, and you'll soon be turning your weaknesses into strengths.

> "Excellence is an art won by training and habituation. We do not act rightly because we have virtue or excellence, but we rather have those because we have acted rightly. We are what we repeatedly do. Excellence, then, is not an act but a habit."
>
> **–Aristotle**

Keep doing the things you're now doing, and you'll keep getting the things you've been getting. So I ask you, does that make you happy? You see, excellence in anything in life comes from repeatedly doing those things that you want to get good at. The things that others talk about but really never do. And when you do something long enough and often enough, you get really good at it. So good, that it'll not only amaze you, but everyone else as well. So if having a great-looking and great-feeling body is something you want, keep at it and don't you dare quit. You're closer than ever to achieving excellence.

36

Forgotten Exercises for Delts and Traps

Ever notice how often your training falls into a rut? Do you find yourself gravitating to the same leg press, press-down, and curl time and time again until you eventually realize that you aren't getting the results you want? Don't worry, all bodybuilders have been there.

Chances are, you're using the same five or six exercises each time you train a body part. With the same stimulus constantly hitting your muscles, no wonder you're in a rut! One of the simplest ways to get back on track is to substitute a few different exercises into your routine.

In this chapter, I'm going to give you a few seldom-used exercises that are guaranteed to get you growing again. One last word: in shoulder training, keep the weights light to moderate and the reps high. The shoulder girdle is easily stimulated and best fatigued with nonstop reps; that's when you'll really feel the burn. Heavy weights not only can induce injury, but invite growth-robbing momentum into the movement. Keep it light.

Incline Bench Lateral

When I first saw pictures of Arnold Schwarzenegger doing this in *The Encyclopedia of Bodybuilding*, I couldn't wait to try it. After a few awkward sets, I found the right groove and could immediately feel the rear delts working in ways I'd never felt before. Here's how to do it:

- Adjust the incline bench to between 20 and 40 degrees.
- Lie on your side against the pad. With your outside hand, grab the dumbbell and extend your arm nearly straight down in front of you. Raise your arm out to your side as if you're doing a lateral raise, maintaining the angle in your elbow at all times. Raise your arm until it's directly above your upper torso.
- At the top of the movement, slightly pronate your wrist so that your little finger is higher.
- Lower the weight under control. Keep constant tension in your delts.

Incline bench lateral (a)

Incline bench lateral (b)

- Start with your weaker delt, then switch arms after you complete all your reps.

INTENSITY TIP: Try descending sets. For example, after completing your first set on one side, immediately pick up a dumbbell that weighs 50 to 75 percent of the first and do another set. Upon finishing, again select a dumbbell 25 to 50 percent lighter and do another set. Repeat on the other side.

Reverse Pec Deck

Do this exercise to isolate the rear delts, a weak area for most bodybuilders. Face the pec deck machine (instead of facing away from it, which you'd do for chest work). Adjust the seat so that your arms are parallel to the floor, not angled up or down. In addition, keep these tips in mind:

- Think of your hands as hooks as you grasp the handles. Don't grip

too tightly, or you'll fatigue your wrists and forearms, causing a premature end to your set. Focus all muscle stimulation on the delts.
- Sit up squarely on the seat with a slight arch in your lower back.
- Keep your elbows up and your arms in a fixed arc throughout the entire range of motion. Don't change the angle of your elbows.
- Use a controlled speed on both the positive and negative contractions. Momentum does nothing for muscle growth.
- Contract the delts for a second as you pull the handles as far out to your sides as you can.
- An excellent variation that allows you to isolate each side is the single-arm version. You may want to position your body facing just slightly to the side you're working. With your free hand, grab the backpad for support.

Reverse pec deck (a)

Reverse pec deck (b)

INTENSITY TIP: To really burn the rear delts, try to raise your elbows as high as possible in the contracted position.

One-Arm Alternate Front Raise

This exercise works the anterior (front) delts, and it can be a real burner. The trick is to keep your delts working by using a continuous motion. As one arm is coming down, the other is just beginning to go up. Follow these tips:

- To do the alternate version, use dumbbells. If you prefer cables, it's easier to do all your reps first with one arm before switching to the other. Try them both to see which you prefer, but include both varieties in your training regimen.
- Keep the weights moving in an even arc by maintaining the angle in your elbows throughout the range of motion. Bring the weights directly in front of you or slightly toward your midline.
- Don't stop at shoulder level. You'll get greater shoulder development—even though it's more difficult—if you bring the weights overhead. Think contraction at the top.
- If you use cables, don't let the weights clank at the bottom, which allows your delts to rest momentarily. Continuous tension is key throughout the range of motion.
- Use a smooth and steady speed. If you bend your knees a little to get the weights up, they're too heavy. You won't ever impress anyone with isolation shoulder exercises that incur injury!

INTENSITY TIP: Avoid shrugging your shoulders upward during this exercise—this can shift emphasis from the delts to the traps.

One-arm alternate front raise (a)

One-arm alternate front raise (b)

Behind-Back Lateral Cable Raise

This is a variation of the lateral cable raise in which you bring your arm in front of your body. This slight change in the angle will target the side delts somewhat differently. I also favor cables over dumbbells because of the smoothness of the movement and the ability to better control the weight and even the resistance throughout the full range of motion. Follow these tips:

- Stand next to a lower cable, facing to the side. Your working delt is the farthest from the weight stack. Reach behind your back for the handle.

- Keeping your upper body erect, raise your arm in a controlled motion to well above shoulder level. Keep the angle of your elbow the same throughout the range of motion. If you stop at

Behind-back lateral cable raise (a)

Behind-back lateral cable raise (b)

shoulder level, you'll limit the benefit of this movement.

- Lower your arm slowly to the lowest point where tension is maintained in the delt. If the weight stack once hits bottom and the tension is released, you've gone too far.
- After you complete your reps for one side, do the other.

INTENSITY TIP: Experiment with body position. When at a right angle to the weight stack, you will primarily work the side delts; facing away from the weight stack, you will focus on the front delts. Try variations in-between.

Front Barbell Raise

This old favorite isolates the front delts. Like the dumbbell and cable alternate front raise, you don't need heavy

weight to get great results. Keep the reps high and nonstop. Some other tips to follow:

- The motion is similar to the one-arm front raise except that you use both arms simultaneously.
- Try cutting your rest time between sets to 30 to 45 seconds. Your delts won't be completely recovered, but that's one good tool to really blitz them.
- Use a variety of grip widths: close (4 to 6 inches apart), medium (8 to 12 inches apart), and wide (outside of hands against the inside of the weight plates).

INTENSITY TIP: For a variation, attach a straight bar to the low cable stack. Facing the weights, perform the movement as you would with a barbell.

Front barbell raise

Front barbell raise—variation (a)

Front barbell raise—variation (b)

Cross-Cable Reverse Flye

This exercise is a tremendous rear-delts burner because it isolates the muscle so effectively. Do this movement standing between two cable weight stacks. Grasp the right upper cable handle with your left hand and the left handle with your right hand.

To add tension in the delts, keep your arms and elbows raised higher than your delts throughout the range of motion. Follow these other tips:

- Be sure to stand midway between the stacks to equalize the angle of tension.
- Don't let the weight stacks touch bottom, which allows your delts to rest. Restrict the range of motion if you have long arms or the weight stacks are placed close together. Once again, continuous tension is the key.
- Maintain the angle in your elbows throughout the range of motion so that your triceps don't become involved in the work.

- With your elbows up, pull the handles across your chest (don't change the angle in your elbows as you do this) and extend your arms as far back behind you as possible, then momentarily squeeze your delts. Keep your body stationary and a slight arch in your lower back.
- Don't count reps, but you should be able to do at least 8. If you can do another rep, do it. If you can do one more—even just a partial rep—do it. Feel the burn!

INTENSITY TIP: This exercise can also be done one arm at a time for complete isolation. Hold onto a cable station upright with your free hand to stabilize your body.

Behind-Back Shrug

Eight-time Mr. Olympia Lee Haney popularized this traps exercise. As the name implies, you do this one with the barbell behind your back using the same straight-up-and-down shrugging

Cross-cable reverse flye (a)

Cross-cable reverse flye (b)

Behind-back shrug (a)   **Behind-back shrug (b)**

movement. Place the barbell slightly below your glutes in a power rack or squat rack. This will help you pick up the weight and return it more easily. Follow these tips:

- Use an overhand grip with your palms facing away from you. Don't expect to go as heavy as you can on shrugs with the bar in front of your body.
- Don't use a rotational movement, just straight-up-and-down reps. With heavy weights, rotational forces create unwanted stress on the delicate shoulder girdle.
- Use a fairly fast speed on the way up, then hold and contract at the top for a second and release slowly.
- Watch yourself in a mirror, particularly your arms. If you see the

angle in your elbows changing as you complete the movement, you're bringing in assisting muscle groups. Concentrate on keeping your arms as straight as possible. Also, keep your head slightly up to help maintain the arch in your back. Don't look down.

- Try to touch your shoulders to your ears on each rep. When you can't do any more full-range reps, do partial reps.
- After you finish this exercise, grab a chinning bar to stretch your lower back. Hang for 10 to 15 seconds to fully extend your body.
- Go heavy: do 5 to 9 reps to build size and strength.

INTENSITY TIP: If your glutes get in the way of the bar, try using dumbbells. Follow the same basic form.

37

No More Mr. Stickman

A Wide Approach for the Broomstick Physique

I've got this friend, bless his heart, who tries really hard to get wide, but he still looks like a broomstick. Imagine how hard it was for me to tell him I've seen bigger delts on a pencil. Okay, okay, I'll erase that comment.

And what kind of friend would I be if I didn't tell him that he most definitely qualifies for a full gym membership refund? You would, too, if folks couldn't tell whether you were standing sideways or frontward. So, what's an O'Cedar kind of guy to do? Get smart and get wide—real wide!

First, let's get smart. If you want wide, you need to do pullups or pulldowns and laterals like a maniac. Pullups or pulldowns are going to widen you like no other movement. Some people say they've tried to get wide but they can't. Tell that to the scores of bodybuilders in their 30s, 40s, and 50s who got serious about pulling and really widened out.

Spreading your wings is one thing; putting meat on is another. Barbell and dumbbell presses most definitely pack mass on delts. But for some reason, some bodybuilders don't get much from them. For them and many others,

the answer, it seems, is laterals—dumbbell laterals.

Laterals use one group of muscles—the delts—to work one group of muscles—the delts. Just doing straight sets of laterals, though, won't cut it. Those pesky delts recover quickly between reps and sets. You need intensity. That means using several of the good ol' Weider Principles I told you about earlier in the book—principles like various rep combos, compound sets, continuous tension, and peak contractions.

Don't do all of these exercises in one workout. Pick two to three one workout, and two or three different ones for the next. Mix it up and have fun!

If you're tired of little or no results, start doing these exercises. However, be warned: save some cash. You'll need it for bigger clothes after 60 days of using these growth producers.

KNOW YOUR DELTS

Before hammering your delts, you should know their anatomy and function. The shoulder is where your arm connects to your shoulder blade. This glenohumeral joint is held together primarily by soft tissues—muscles, tendons, and ligaments. A balance of flexibility, strength, and development will help you avoid injury to this vulnerable area.

The deltoid is a three-headed muscle—front, middle, and rear—and is the primary abductor of the arm. (Abduction is the movement that brings the arm up and away from the body.) The rotator cuff is a series of smaller muscles that originate on the scapula and control rotation of the arm, helping to provide stability to the joint.

Since internal rotation is inherently stronger because of the number of muscles contributing to this action, bodybuilders who neglect their external rotators are asking for trouble. The solution is to do 3 sets of light dumbbell external rotations before heavy delts training. Keep these other points in mind:

- Proper external rotation requires that shoulder joints to upper arms and elbow joints form 90-degree angles.
- Improper external rotation commonly includes relaxed, lowered shoulder girdle, and elbows lowered and behind the body. In addition, the arms are moving forward and away from the vertical.
- Because muscles that use internal rotation (like pecs and lats) can become much stronger than the supporting muscle structure, common sense should be used.
- Prevent anterior shoulder instability, imbalance, and injury of the rotator cuff by equally developing all heads (front, side, and rear) of the delts, along with pecs and lats.

SOME GREAT EXERCISES AND COMBINATIONS

Standing One-Arm Dumbbell Press and Heavy Dumbbell Partial Side Lateral

Start with the one-arm press. Take a weight you can press for 7 to 10 reps and stand erect. Lower the dumbbell to shoulder level, and press up until the arm is fully locked. Lower the weight and repeat for the other side.

With minimal rest, quickly move to heavy dumbbell standing partial-rep side laterals. Choose a weight that's at least twice as heavy as you'd normally use for regular side laterals. Keep your arms locked and hold the weight out to your side, then raise the weight up as far as you can with your arms still completely locked. Do as many reps as possible. Keep doing reps until you can no longer move the weight; the trick is not to rest between reps. Keep those reps going nonstop, even if you're able to move the weight up only an inch or so. Do 3 to 5 compound sets.

Wide Pullup or Pulldown

Take a grip 8 to 12 inches wider than your shoulders. Lower your body until your arms are fully extended. Bend your knees and cross your feet behind you. Pull yourself up until the bar touches your upper chest, squeeze the lats hard, then lower yourself slowly and repeat. Be sure to pull yourself up to at least chin level. Do 3 sets of as many reps as you can do.

If you can't do pullups right now, do pulldowns. Do them two ways, using both overhand and underhand grips. With the overhand grip, use the same grip position as wide chins. With the underhand grip, keep your hands four to six inches apart, and as you pull the bar down, pull your elbows back and behind you. In both movements, keep a slight arch in your back. Do three sets to failure, about 10 to 15 reps.

Dumbbell Pendulum-Style Side Lateral

This is probably different than what you've been doing. Before you begin, practice the movement. Keep your upper torso erect and both arms down at your sides. Raise your left arm up to shoulder level and directly out to the side of your torso.

Slowly lower the left arm; and as you do, begin raising the right arm out from your right side. Raise it to shoulder level, lower, and repeat. The movement is like a pendulum; back and forth, nonstop.

Keep this going for 12 to 20 reps each side. You won't be able to use much of anything that resembles a heavy weight, but that's okay. The focus of this exercise is slow, intense delt contractions from beginning to end using slow, continuous tension that will cause a terrific burn.

Wide-Grip Upright Row

The wider the grip, the less weight you can use, but the more it works your side delts. Take an overhand grip at least six to eight inches wider than your shoulders. Bring your arms up until the bar is roughly chest level.

At the top of the exercise, keep your elbows higher than the bar and your wrists locked. Slowly lower the bar and repeat. Go for 12 to 15 reps, and forget the heavy weight. Go for the burn and picture-perfect reps. Experiment by finding what height (how high you bring the bar up) maximally contracts the delts while minimally using the biceps.

"O Lord, thou givest us everything, at the price of an effort."

—Leonardo da Vinci

That's all it takes—just a little effort—to change the way you look and feel and your life. So doesn't it just amaze you to no end how many people won't even do that? I mean, it's so simple for folks to look and feel great, and all it takes is a little effort on their part, and the body will do the rest. Geez, it doesn't get much easier than that. But, as you know, most people would rather talk about something than do it. However, I'm willing to bet big money that that isn't you. You know that if you want a great body, all you have to do is work out, eat right, get enough rest, keep your stress levels low, and enjoy your life—and amazingly, your body will do the rest. Way to go, friend. I'm happy you've learned such a simple truth!

38

Forgotten Back Exercises That *Work*!

Just as you would never hit your chest from only one angle, the same goes for back training. Zero in on the upper-outer lats to develop the sought-after V-shape, the middle back for tremendous thickness, and the lower back to bring out your "Christmas tree."

Lats, the popular term for the latissimus dorsi muscles, are not just a single muscle, but actually part of an ensemble of muscles, including the erector spinae, teres major and minor, infraspinatus, rhomboids, and trapezius muscles.

Such a powerful collection of muscles needs more stimulation than just behind-neck pulldowns and seated rows to develop awe-inspiring force: you need a variety of movements, each targeting a slightly different area. Check out these forgotten back exercises—they're guaranteed to bridge the gap from your current back development to where you want it to be.

One last word on reps: if you want to get growing, discontinue the 10-reps-per-set scheme here and now. The back is a strong muscle group; hit it with very heavy weights (that still allow you to use good form) so that you reach muscular failure at 6, 7, or even 8 reps. As you get stronger and can do more reps, add more weight.

One-Arm Standing Cable Row

This lat builder requires precise form to keep the delts from doing much of the work. Use a full range of motion for best results. Always think big stretch at the bottom, and pull back as far as you can at the top and contract. Follow these other tips:

- Stand turned slightly away from the low-cable apparatus; the leg opposite your working arm should be one step in front of the other. Bend your knees and lean slightly forward.
- Grasp a stirrup cable handle, and position your body far enough away from the pulley that you can completely extend your working arm to stretch the lat.
- Pull your arm back as far behind you as possible, keeping your elbow close to your body. Focus on making the back contract.

One-arm standing cable row (a)

One-arm standing cable row (b)

- Slowly lower the weight, allowing your arm to fully extend to get that extra stretch.
- For added intensity, do drop sets by reducing the weight when you hit momentary muscle failure. Don't rest too long—doing so reduces the intensity.
- Do a complete set with one arm before working the other.

INTENSITY TIP: The elbow comes away from the body when the hand is kept in a neutral or pronated position, more effectively targeting the teres and rhomboid muscles. Supination allows the elbow to stay closer to the body, which works the lower lat to a greater degree.

Two-Arm Standing Cable Row

This can be done with an overhand grip, but the reverse grip gives me a better feel. I also use a curved bar rather than a straight bar because it puts less stress on the biceps, and therefore more on the lats. Stand far enough away from the weight stack so that you can fully extend your arms and stretch the lats. More guidelines:

- Lean forward at a 60- to 80-degree angle.
- Pull your arms back, making sure you keep your elbows close to the sides of your body. The farther you bring your arms back, the more fully you contract your back.
- For a super pump, do one to two drop sets on your last set.

One-Arm Seated Row

You've no doubt done the seated cable row—a very effective exercise—with both arms. This time, try working one arm at a time to isolate each side (you

Two-arm standing cable row (a)

Two-arm standing cable row (b)

One-arm seated row (a)

One-arm seated row (b)

won't be able to use as much weight, so try just less than half of what you normally use).

One key benefit: working your arms independently forces each side to do all the work; a stronger opposite lat can't overpower the weaker one. Then follow these tips:

- Keep your knees slightly bent and a slight arch in your lower back. Lean forward at the waist no more than about 10 degrees.
- Place your nonworking hand on top of your thigh.
- Don't rotate your body as you complete the movement. Keep the

form strict by facing forward throughout the range of motion.

- Feel your lats stretch as you lower the weight, almost as if it's coming around to the side.
- Complete a set with one arm before working the other.

Close-Grip Pullup

This effectively develops the intercostal and lower-lat tie-in. (As an alternative to the straight-bar variety, two-time Mr. Olympia Franco Columbu did these with his palms facing each other and a V-bar placed over the horizontal pullup bar.) Additional tips to follow:

- Use an overhand grip and keep your hands spaced about 6 to 8 inches apart.
- Pull your body up to the bar until it reaches your chest. Avoid swinging and using muscle-robbing momentum to get your body up.

Close-grip pullup (a)

Close-grip pullup (b)

- Lower your body under control until your arms are fully extended.
- Do partial reps when you can no longer do full-range reps.
- If you can't do at least 5 good reps, use a machine that assists you with the movement.

Straight-Arm Pulldown

Do this movement, which approximates the feel of a straight-arm dumbbell pullover across a flat bench, to really target the lower-lat tie-in. A lot of bodybuilders use too much weight and, as a result, can't do it with proper form. Bad form doesn't equal good results. The keys to making this a great exercise are:

- On a cable pulldown or triceps pressdown apparatus, place your hands about 12 inches apart on a straight bar.
- Maintain a slight bend in your knees and lean forward about 10 to 30 degrees at the waist.
- Extend your arms out in front of you. The angle in your elbows won't change from this position.
- Establishing the mind–muscle link, press the bar down until your arms are by your sides. Use a controlled movement, and squeeze the lats at the point of peak contraction.
- Allow the bar to slowly rise up higher than your head at the top of the movement.

Reverse-Grip Pulldown

This is one of the most effective high-to-low lat exercises you can do. The most important point here is to pull your arms down and far behind you for a hard contraction. The fully extended arm position at the top also allows you to really stretch your lats. Follow these other tips:

- The underhand grip—with your hands spaced about six to eight inches apart—is what sets this

Straight-arm pulldown (a)

Straight-arm pulldown (b)

Reverse-grip pulldown (a)

Reverse-grip pulldown (b)

pulldown movement apart. This subtle change provides significant results.

- Compared to an overhand grip, the underhand grip will let you use heavier weight. After a good warm-up, go as heavy as possible, but always use good form.
- Keep your upper torso arched as you pull the bar down, but don't arch too much (this will take the work off the back and put more on the biceps).
- Do the movement in a controlled motion. Too much momentum enables you to lift more weight and do a greater number of reps, but provides little muscle stimulation.
- Think peak contraction.

Incline Bench Dumbbell Row (Lying Face Down)

A good variation on an already great movement. Follow these tips for best results:

- Lie facedown on an incline bench elevated between 30 and 45 degrees.

- With a dumbbell in each hand, bring your elbows straight behind you for a maximal peak contraction.
- Lower the weights until your arms are fully extended. Go for that extra inch or so of stretch, but keep the shoulders stabilized.

Incline Bench Dumbbell Row (One Leg Kneeling)

This version is also done on an incline bench, but you place one knee on the seat and stand with the other foot on the floor. Further guidelines to follow:

- Hold on to the top of the back pad with your nonworking arm for support, and lean forward about 60 to 80 degrees.
- Get ready; this movement requires a strong mind–muscle link.
- Lower the dumbbell until your arm is fully extended and your lat is stretched, then bring your arm straight up and your elbow behind you as far as possible.
- Always go for a deep stretch and intense contraction.

Incline bench dumbbell row (lying face down) (a)

Incline bench dumbbell row (lying face down) (b)

Incline bench dumbbell row (one leg kneeling) (a)

Incline bench dumbbell row (one leg kneeling) (b)

Reverse Hyper

Creating a strong lower back, which can often be the weakest link of the body, should be one of your top training priorities. A strong lower back will also help prevent injury by allowing you to squat, press, and deadlift more effectively.

Deadlifts, both stiff-legged and regular, are probably the best way to develop a strong lower back. Reverse hypers are also very effective. Remember: as with all low-back exercises, be sure to warm up thoroughly, work up in weight slowly, and don't overtrain the lower back; once a week for deadlifts and twice a week for hypers. Then follow these tips:

- Place the barbell across your upper traps (as in squatting) and keep your feet shoulder-width apart and pointing forward.
- With your knees nearly locked, lean forward at the waist in a slow and controlled manner until you form a 90-degree angle.
- Keep your head up and in line with your back as you rise up. Concentrate; think low-back muscles as you contract the erectors.
- Return to the fully upright position.

Spider Bench Row

One version of the spider bench that's available in most gyms has a foot platform and a small pad to support the upper torso. Other spider benches have a T-bar that can be plate-loaded. Whichever you choose, be sure to do the following:

Reverse hyper (a)

Reverse hyper (b)

Spider bench row (a)

Spider bench row (b)

- Position your upper torso so that the top of the bench pad comes no higher than the bottom of your chest. This gives you a better lat stretch.
- As you raise the barbell or T-bar, bring your arms as far back behind you as possible to fully contract your back. It's okay to raise your upper body off the pad a few inches and slightly arch your back for maximal contraction.

- Keep your head up. This will ensure that you don't round your back, a potentially dangerous thing, especially when fatigue starts to set in.
- Lower the weight until your arms are fully extended. Keep your shoulders stabilized, but be sure to give the lats a full stretch.
- Don't bounce or jerk the weight. The movement is slow and controlled from start to finish.

39

Forgotten Exercises for Biceps

Who doesn't want big guns? To build 'em, I sincerely hope you're doing more than standing barbell curls—because relying on only one main exercise will develop, well, just pistols. Let's talk about truly monstrous-sized arms—cannons. To get you there, I've scoured the nation's gyms to find some growth-promoting exercises that'll add spark to your biceps training.

Here's some advice on reps: do mass-building movements at the beginning of your biceps routine and keep reps in the 6 to 10 range. Do isolation and peaking exercises with lighter weights toward the end of your biceps workout in the 8 to 12 range.

But don't get hung up on numbers, like doing all sets to 10 reps. Take some to 20, others to 5. Keep mixing it up. Try out some of these "forgotten" movements—surefire hope for puny arms. It's time to get growing again.

Lying-Flat Bench Dumbbell Curl

When was the last time you did a biceps exercise lying down? If you want a good mass-building *and* peaking movement, this one's hard to beat. Experiment with elbow angle, because therein lies the secret to its effectiveness. You'll need a

flat bench that's high enough to allow your arms to fully extend below the bench without the weights touching the floor. Follow these other tips:

- With a dumbbell in each hand, keep your palms turned up (supinated) throughout the movement.
- Keep your upper arm angled at roughly 45 degrees to your torso, but experiment with various angles to find which one hits your biceps best.
- Try to keep your upper arm in about the same position throughout the exercise. Movement takes place through only the bend in your elbows.
- At the top, squeeze and hold the peak contraction for a one-two count, then slowly lower the weight.
- You can curl both arms at a time or alternate sides.

TIP FOR BIG ARMS: Use light weights with this excellent finishing movement. Go for a good stretch at the bottom (use only a raised flat bench). Supinate and squeeze the biceps.

Lying-flat bench dumbbell curl (a)

Lying-flat bench dumbbell curl (b)

Lying Cable Curl (Elbows Elevated)

Ever see a water skier waiting in position, ski tips up and leaning back? You'll start this movement in a similar position. Sit down in front of a weight stack with a straight or curved bar (in a rotating sleeve) attached to the low cable. Keep your body square (the cable should follow your midline) and lie back.

- Allow your arms to fully extend before beginning the exercise.
- With your elbows raised above your upper torso, curl the weight and bring the bar back toward your face until your biceps are fully contracted.
- Experiment with elbow angle and the distance you bring the bar

Lying cable curl (a)

Lying cable curl (b)

back so that you can maximally contract your biceps.

- Slowly lower the weight until your arms are fully extended. Keep your elbows above your upper torso from start to finish.

TIP FOR BIG ARMS: This movement allows you to hit your biceps from a new angle, and is especially effective over the bottom third of the range of motion. Momentum is minimized because you're lying on the floor.

Standing Two-Arm Cable Curl

If your gym's cable crossover unit isn't wide enough for you to stand in the center and fully extend your arms without the plates hitting the stacks, simply take a few steps backward or forward. But that's only the beginning.

- Keep your arms elevated and parallel to the floor as you curl your

hands toward your elbows just slightly to fully contract the biceps.

- Extend your arms under control to full extension.
- For variety, do a rep by bringing your elbows in and supinating your hands at the top.

TIP FOR BIG ARMS: Try down-the-rack (strip set) training with this finishing movement, pulling the pins and lowering the weight after you reach muscular failure.

Zottman Curl

You sure don't see many bodybuilders doing these anymore. Too bad. Zottman curls build powerful forearm, biceps, and brachialis muscles. The key is the hand and dumbbell position on the return to the start position. Here's how to do them:

Standing two-arm cable curl (a)

Standing two-arm cable curl (b)

Zottman curl (a)

Zottman curl (b)

Zottman curl (c)

Zottman curl (d)

- Use a pair of moderately heavy dumbbells. After 6 reps, you'll really feel your arms working.
- Stand with your arms close to your sides. With palms up, curl both arms until your biceps are fully contracted.

- At the point of peak contraction, turn your palms down and keep them in this position as you move your arms to full extension.
- On the downward portion, turn your arms so that the weights are lowered at an angle away from the

midline of your body. This gives
the biceps a better stretch.

TIP FOR BIG ARMS: The first half of the
movement is a lot like a standing
dumbbell curl—but when you reach
the point of peak contraction, pronate
your hands and turn your arms slightly
out to your sides before lowering the
weight. This action targets the biceps
differently, and builds powerful forearms as well.

Spider Bench Curl

Nowadays, most spider benches are
used for supported T-bar rowing. If you
don't have access to a spider bench,
you can also use an incline bench set at
a fairly low angle.

Spider bench curl (a)

- Lie high enough on the bench so
  that you can curl the weight up
  without hitting the top of the
  bench. Once in position, have a
  partner give you an EZ-bar (or barbell). Try a variety of grip widths
  to hit slightly different areas of
  the muscle.
- On one set, keep your upper arms
  completely vertical as you raise
  and lower the weight. On your
  next set, allow your elbows to
  come forward as you curl the
  weight. Still another variation:
  bring your elbows in. Make note
  of how each position feels.
- If you allow your head to drop as
  you curl the weight, you can bring
  the weight up even farther—
  behind your head—for a super
  contraction.
- Try using dumbbells for an
  entirely different feeling.
- Lower the weight slowly, and fully
  extend your arms.
- Skip the cheat movements here;
  keep it strict.

Spider bench curl (b)

Spider bench curl (c)

TIP FOR BIG ARMS: This movement somewhat resembles a preacher curl on a spider or incline bench. A variety of

Spider bench curl–
alternate grip

grips—even using dumbbells—allows
you to hit your biceps from all angles.
Try partial reps after you reach full-rep
failure.

Lying Overhead Cable Curl

This is a great peaking movement popular among many past bodybuilding
champs. You'll like the smoothness and
even tension in the biceps from start to
finish. Use a handle with a rotating
sleeve, preferably a curved one for a
better grip. Additional tips:

- Position a flat bench directly
  under a high pulley. Your head
  goes closest to the cable.

- Extend your arms straight up so
  that your upper arms are nearly
  parallel to the cable support column. Lock your upper arms in this
  position throughout the exercise.
- Curl the bar toward and just
  behind your head; this will put
  the biceps in the fully contracted
  position.
- Forcefully contract and squeeze
  your biceps for one count.
- Slowly bring the bar up, and fully
  extend your arms for a complete
  stretch.

TIP FOR BIG ARMS: The great bodybuilding champs of the 1970s regularly

Lying overhead cable curl (a)   Lying overhead cable curl (b)

made use of this superior peaking exercise. It provides maximal tension over the last half of the range of motion. Use a bar with a rotating sleeve to keep the pressure off the wrists.

Barbell Pole Curl

A barbell curl is a barbell curl, right? Not exactly. You'll have to try this movement to know what I mean. It's like a regular barbell curl, except that you lean firmly against a pole or wall during the entire exercise. Talk about intensity!

- Don't expect to use the same weight as a regular barbell curl. Lighten the load.
- Keep your head and upper torso firmly against the pole throughout

the range of motion. Don't let your back come off the surface even an inch!
- Use wide, medium, and close grips to target specific areas of the biceps.
- Keep your elbows locked at your sides—don't let them come up and in front of your torso.

TIP FOR BIG ARMS: Regular standing barbell curls use a lot of momentum— more than you realize you're giving. This movement takes out all extraneous movement, zeroing in on the biceps. Use about two-thirds of the weight you can handle with standing curls. Bring the weight all the way up for a peak contraction.

Barbell pole curl (a)

Barbell pole curl (b)

"Why have you settled for so little when you can have so much?"

I'm telling you right now that you can have whatever you want in life, if you'll only believe you can have it and give up the belief that you can't. It may not come immediately; few things ever do, especially the things we cherish most. But if you keep at it, you'll achieve whatever you want, if it's something you deeply desire. Don't accept the bread crumbs that other people will leave for you by not going for your dreams and your heart's desire. Go for it all and accept nothing less, because you deserve it!

40

Forgotten Exercises for Triceps

Big arms mean big biceps, right? Yeah, but if you spend a disproportionate amount of time working on beach muscles like your biceps, you're making a big mistake. Many bodybuilders put too much emphasis on the biceps, when in reality the triceps make up roughly two-thirds of your upper-arm size. The fact is, if you want big arms—sleeve-busting arms—you need to work your triceps hard, too.

The lateral and medial heads of the triceps extend the forearm at the elbow, while the long head adducts the arm. Exercise selection and angle of movement are therefore important considerations in your attempt to hit all three heads. That's what I've got for you here: long-forgotten triceps exercises not often done.

One word on reps: do 6 to 8 for mass-building movements, and, if you feel like a change of pace, 10 to 15. Most triceps exercises require very strict form, because doing them incorrectly—like the guy who does press-downs with his entire body leaning over the cable—invites too much delt involvement.

Strap Overhead Extension

Anytime you lean forward at the waist and extend your arms overhead, you work the long head of the triceps. Two-time Mr. Olympia Larry Scott told me that this exercise helped him develop tremendous triceps size. Here's how to do it:

- Attach a strap (or rope) handle to a cable on a high pulley. Facing away from the cable apparatus, grasp the strap and pull it over your head.
- With a slight bend in your knees, lean forward at the waist (about 60 to 80 degrees). For balance, you might want to keep one foot in front of the other.
- Move your arms up by the sides of your head, and your hands near your forehead.
- Keep your upper arms and elbows in a fixed position throughout the movement. Extend the strap as far as possible in front of you, fully extending your arms.
- When you reach full extension, turn your wrists out (pronation) so

Strap overhead extension (a)

Strap overhead extension (b)

the palms face down. This will amplify the triceps contraction.

One-Arm Cable Extension
The beauty of this movement is that you can really feel the muscle work—almost like a concentration curl. Follow these tips:

- Attach a stirrup handle to a high pulley cable. Grasp the handle with one hand, and face away from the cable apparatus.
- Place your nonworking hand on the biceps of your working arm. Keep it there to stabilize the upper arm.
- With the cable coming over the opposite shoulder and your knuckles just in front of your face, lean forward at the waist about 45 degrees. Now you're ready to start.

- Using an overhand grip, keep your elbow stationary and press to full extension. Go for a peak contraction, momentarily squeezing the muscle in that position.
- Let the weight stack pull your hand back toward your opposite shoulder under full control.

Flat Bench Dip
Time to get heavy. You've probably done dips before, but this movement is excellent for developing your triceps just above the elbow. It's a good choice for a first exercise in your routine. Start with only your body weight as resistance, and soon you'll be adding a 45-pound plate (have a partner place it on top of your thighs, not across your knees).

- Position two flat benches about three feet apart. Hold onto the

One-arm cable extension (a)

One-arm cable extension (b)

Flat bench dip (a)

Flat bench dip (b)

long edge of one bench (arms and hands by your sides, palms facing away), then place one heel on top of the other. Adjust the spacing between the benches, if necessary.

- To descend, bend your elbows slowly. Your elbows should point straight behind you, not out to your sides.
- Go down as far as possible. For better leverage and stability, keep your back close to the edge of the bench. Press back up with your triceps; feel the contraction.
- When you can do no more than 15 reps without much trouble, have your partner place a weight plate across your quads.

One-Arm Reverse-Grip Pressdown

You know how to do this good ol' pressdown: upper arms and elbows close to your sides, hands move no higher than chest level, and a powerful lockout and contraction at the bottom. This time, you're going to do it with an underhand grip—called a reverse grip— with a stirrup handle on the cable machine. Though it can be done with both arms simultaneously, working each arm independently allows you to really feel the muscle.

- Some bodybuilders recommend facing the weight stack; others suggest turning sideways. Try both variations to see which works best for you.
- With a palms-up grip and your elbow firmly by your side, straighten your arm at a moderate rate of speed until it's completely extended.
- Hold the peak contraction, then let your arm come back up slowly.
- Keep your hand in line with your forearm; don't flex the wrist during the movement.
- To work the lateral head more, stabilize your upper arm. If your

One-arm reverse-grip pressdown (a)

One-arm reverse-grip pressdown (b)

upper arm moves forward and back, the long head is involved to a greater degree.

Close-Grip Bench Press

And you thought the bench press was only for building massive pecs! That it does, but with just a couple of adjustments, it also builds thick triceps muscles.

- Reduce the starting weight to about 50 percent of what you'd use on a fairly heavy set of regular bench presses.

- Place your hands 6 to 10 inches apart. Hand position is the key to greater triceps involvement, so experiment to find one that really smokes your arms.

- Starting with the barbell just below your chest, push up (try to keep your elbows from flaring out too far) to full extension.

- Lower the weight under control, then press right back up.

Close-grip bench press (a)

Close-grip bench press (b)

One-Arm Dumbbell French Press

This exercise is a terrific triceps shaper. For this version, as for the two-hand dumbbell version, be sure to thoroughly warm up the tendons that connect to the triceps and your elbow.

- Choose a weight that you can handle for 10 to 12 reps in good form.
- Sit on the edge of a flat bench, keeping your upper torso erect, and bring the weight above your head.
- With your free hand, you may support the elbow of your working arm to keep your upper arm stationary.
- Allow the weight to come down behind your head, getting a good stretch of the triceps.

- Straighten your arm to raise the weight back up, contracting your triceps at lockout.

Two-Arm Barbell Kickback

Once you do this exercise, you'll call it a real triceps burner. This great finishing movement will bring out triceps detail.

- Many bodybuilders use only the weight of a 45-pound Olympic bar. If you can lift more than that, you're in good company.
- Position the bar behind you, then squat down and pick it up. Your palms should face away from you.
- With your legs close together and knees bent slightly, lean forward (60 to 80 degrees) so that the weight comes to slightly higher than your knees.

One-arm dumbbell French press (a)

One-arm dumbbell French press (b)

- Keep your upper arms and elbows close to your torso from start to finish.
- Fully extend and lock out your arms behind you, holding the weight for a count. It'll be hard, but really contract your triceps.
- Slowly lower the bar and repeat. You'll be lucky to get 6 reps, but do as many as you can.

Two-arm barbell kickback

41

Forgotten Exercises for Chest

Today's bodybuilders have access to a greater number of high-tech machines than ever, but the movement away from basic freeweight exercises isn't a good sign. Few can dispute that the greatest chest in the sport belonged to Arnold Schwarzenegger, who ruled the bodybuilding world in the early 1970s.

Take a look at some of those early photos, and you'll see pec thickness and mass like that of no other. While Arnold may have been genetically endowed in the chest department, he still trained his Austrian glutes off. And the cornerstone of his workout included heavy, basic movements—benches, flyes, and dips.

Yet those of us who've done nothing but the basics would like a little variety in our routines. For that reason, I've researched some forgotten chest exercises that may just be the spark you need to make a good chest an incredible one!

One word on reps: for compound movements like presses, work in the 6- to 10-rep range, which is best for building size and strength. Do assistance exercises like flyes at the end of your chest routine, and don't be afraid to lighten up on the weight and go for 10 to 15 reps. That really emphasizes the burn.

Close-Hand Push-Up

Here's an exercise you can even do at home, because you don't need any special equipment. I'm sure you're familiar with push-ups, but by simply changing the angle, you work the pecs in different ways. Here's how:

- Use a flat bench or chair at least 18 inches high. Squat down in front of it and then put your feet up on the bench. Your hands and the front of your upper body will rest on the floor.
- Place your hands—one on top of the other—under your lower chest.
- Keeping your body perfectly rigid, press up until you can lock out your arms.
- Slowly lower yourself and repeat. Go to failure.

Close-hand push-up (a)

Close-hand push-up (b)

- To increase resistance, raise your feet even higher. If the movement is too difficult, use a lower bench. This is a fabulous finishing exercise, and works especially well as the second exercise in a compound set.

TIP FOR BIG CHEST: Do the push-up after your chest has been partially fatigued—otherwise it's too easy. Keep your hands directly under your lower chest; if you put your hands too far forward, you'll work your triceps more. Don't stop at failure; do partial reps over the top half of the range of motion.

Bench Cable Flye

Flyes are great for shaping the chest. They're usually done with dumbbells, but in this exercise, you're going to do them with cables. Cables are a terrific alternative, because they give you a different feel and let you train at slightly differing angles—even within the same set—while minimizing shoulder stress and injury. Here's how to do them:

- Position a flat or incline bench between two low pulleys.
- Grasp a stirrup handle in each hand, then lie down on the bench so that your lower chest is in line with the pulleys.
- Keep your palms up and, with a very slight bend in your elbows, bring the handles above your chest.
- To keep constant tension in your chest, don't let your hands touch. Slowly lower your arms until they reach chest level.

TIP FOR BIG CHEST: Cables are better than dumbbells in giving a constant tension throughout the range of motion. Always squeeze your pecs at the top of the movement.

Weighted Dip

Most gyms today have a set of dip bars either by themselves or attached to a chin-up station. Yesterday's great gyms had a separate dipping station with long bars that went from wide to narrow. Talk about hitting your chest and

Bench cable flye (a)

Bench cable flye (b)

Weighted dip (a)

Weighted dip (b)

Decline dumbbell press (a)

Decline dumbbell press (b)

triceps hard—especially with a dumb-bell strapped to and hanging from your waist. This will really make those pecs grow. Do them like this:

- Be sure to warm up your elbows and shoulders before you start. A few light sets of presses and press-downs will do the trick.
- Place your hands on the dip bars, facing inward.
- Keep your upper body upright and your triceps and elbows close to your upper body.
- Experiment with leg position: straight up and down, or bent with your feet crossed and behind you. Which feels better?
- Lower your body as far as possible for a good stretch, but don't go too far. Press back upward, making the triceps and chest do the work.

TIP FOR BIG CHEST: Strap a dumbbell to your waist once the movement becomes easy. If your body weight alone is too heavy, use a machine that takes off part of the load.

Decline Dumbbell Press

If you're accustomed to doing this movement with a barbell, keep in mind that dumbbells offer a greater range of motion and allow a noticeably better contraction in your chest.

Many bodybuilders do decline presses incorrectly, decreasing the range of motion by lowering the dumbbells to their lower chest rather than the upper pecs, just under their chin. If you use heavy weights, have a spotter hand you the dumbbells once you get into position. Once there, here's the best way to do them:

- Don't squirm and move in an effort to get the weights up. Keep your body stationary and your head looking straight up.
- As you lower the weight, keep your elbows pointing straight down, not back.

- Allow the tops of the dumbbells to come below the top of your chest.
- Forcefully push the weights back up in a wide arc, but don't let the dumbbells bang together at the top. Keep them about four to eight inches apart. Controlling the weight keeps constant tension in your pecs.

TIP FOR BIG CHEST: Probably the most difficult aspect of the decline dumbbell press is getting the weights in the ready position and letting them down when you're through. Don't drop the weights when you're finished. That's third-class behavior that doesn't show others or the gym proper respect for the equipment.

Vertical Bench Press Machine

I'd like to offer an exception to my earlier statement about high-tech machines. This piece of equipment can be an excellent chest developer, though it doesn't replace freeweight move-ments. The key here is hand and elbow position. Do it like this:

- Adjust the seat height so you grip the bar at low- to mid-chest level.
- Keep your back firmly against the vertical backpad.
- Throughout the movement, keep your elbows perpendicular to your body.
- Push the bar forward, almost to complete lockout, and really squeeze your pecs.
- As you lower the weight, elevate and push out your chest slightly.
- Many machines offer slight variations in hand position. Try them all to determine which feels best.
- Do controlled nonstop reps.
- Finish off your set with 2 to 3 partial reps, moving the bar only a few inches. What a burn!

TIP FOR BIG CHEST: Though not a perfect substitute for the bench press, the machine version can finish off your pump at the end of your chest workout.

Vertical bench press machine (a)

Vertical bench press machine (b)

Vertical bench press
machine—alternate hand
position

"If you deliberately plan to be less than you are capable of being,
then I warn you, that you will be unhappy for the rest of your life.
You will be evading your own capacities and possibilities."

–Dr. Abraham Maslow

You cheat yourself by accepting less than you're truly capable of. When you do that, it's like lying to the best friend you'll ever have—because that friend is yourself. Don't you dare do that, because there's not one good reason in the world why you should. Think back with me for a moment to a time when you really gave something everything inside of you. Yeah, it may have been incredibly tough, but look how you felt after it was all over. You felt great because you gave your all! And you know what else? That experience made you grow more rapidly than anything that you ever did before it. Always give everything your very best, and push yourself to grow a little bit every day, and you'll be amazed at how quickly you'll grow in every area of your life.

PART VI

All About Excuses, Layoffs, and Injuries

42

Blastin' Through Roadblocks

All Those Excuses

The weather's beautiful as you drive along enjoying the scenery in what seems to be a perfect day. Around every bend in the road, a new vista opens up. You wonder what's around the next turn.

Suddenly you screech to a stop. It's a roadblock. Is this the end of the journey, or do you look for an alternate route? Your answer may give you a good indication of how you respond to roadblocks in your weight training.

Let's face it. Experiencing great training results all the time would be incredible. Some people do; others only wish. Just what are some of the biggest training roadblocks that bodybuilders face? I've listed seven here that I hear most frequently. Let's see if we can't crash through these training roadblocks and continue our journey to great training results.

ROADBLOCK 1

"MY WORKOUTS ARE BORING"

This one is put up by those who do the same exercises, sets, reps, and workouts

all the time. The body and the mind get stale very quickly—and by now, you've heard that enough from me that I know it's sinking in. The body has an amazing ability to adapt quickly to the training demands placed upon it. Crash through this roadblock by changing your exercises, weights, sets, reps, and rest every workout.

ROADBLOCK 2

"I'M NOT GROWING"

This is common among those who overtrain and don't give their bodies enough rest. The body is not a machine that can be trained in the exact same way every workout—or, for that matter, on the exact same days. Some days you'll be stronger than others.

Some workouts will make you sore and more fatigued than others. Crash through this roadblock by listening to your body and giving it the extra rest it needs whenever it needs it.

ROADBLOCK 3

"MY BODY HAS LOOKED THE SAME FOR YEARS"

You may encounter this roadblock if you train with low intensity. Like those who experience the first roadblock, these people just go through the motions in the gym. Their bodies have become so used to their training routine that they stopped growing and getting stronger years ago.

What's needed are high-intensity workouts: heavy weight and slightly longer rest periods; moderate weight with brief rest periods; supersets, tri-sets, giant sets, rest–pause, triple drops. Keep the body constantly off-guard, and it will grow, get stronger, and look better.

ROADBLOCK 4

"I HAVE LITTLE ENERGY"

This is put up by those people who underestimate the importance of nutrition in their diets. Far too many people eat two or three gut-busting meals a day and think that they did their job nutritionally for the day. Wrong! The body must be fed in a specific way to get a specific, predictable result. Crash through this roadblock by:

- Eating four to six small meals per day
- Eating your biggest meal in the morning and gradually tapering down to the smallest meal at night
- Keeping your calories at 50 percent carbs, 35 percent protein, and 15 percent fat
- Having a 50- to 75-gram carb-replacement drink within 30 minutes after training and eating a protein meal within 90 minutes after your workout
- Drinking at least 80 ounces of water per day

ROADBLOCK 5

"I DON'T HAVE ACCESS TO A GOOD GYM OR EQUIPMENT"

Not everyone trains at a gym or has expensive home equipment. Many of the world's bodybuilding champions began training at home with only a barbell and bench. You would be amazed at the results you can achieve with a basic barbell/dumbbell set.

Spend your money wisely and buy one good barbell set (that can also be used for dumbbells) and bench. And you don't even need barbells or machines to do one of the very best calf routines I've found—high-rep calf raises (at least 100 reps nonstop) on the stairs!

ROADBLOCK 6

"I CAN WORK OUT ONLY TWICE A WEEK"

Think you need to work out three or four times per week to get great results? Wrongo, bucko! Remember this: it's not how often you are in the gym that counts. The thing that matters is what you do when you're there! Instead of making excuses:

- Split your workouts into two parts, working half your body one workout, the other half the next. (Thus, you train your whole body only one time per week.)
- Give every workout, set, and rep, 100 percent intensity.
- Keep the number of sets to 8 or fewer for big muscle groups (legs, chest, and back) and 6 or fewer for small muscle groups (shoulders, abs, and arms).

ROADBLOCK 7

"I HAVE TOO MANY INJURIES"

Some people haven't fully shed old ideas of how their bodies should be trained. The belief that there is only one correct way to train your body is a myth. To work around injuries:

- Eliminate those old exercises, sloppy form, weights, and work-outs that initially caused your injury.

- Use new exercises, and develop workouts based upon your present condition and current goals.
- Start slowly, building your range of motion gradually, and accept the idea that you will progress— even if it means slowly.

The body is not a machine that can be trained in the same exact way every workout. Remember that, and you'll go far!

43

On the Road Again

Eating and Training Away from Home

Your workouts are going great. Your strength is up, and you're growing. Is there any better feeling? But wait—you say that you have to go out of town? Are you concerned that your progress will be doomed? Will missing a few days or even a week of regular workouts erase all those gains you've been making?

The good news is that it won't, so relax and chill out. If you time it right, a vacation or business trip can be the perfect prescription for a hard body that needs regular rest. To make the most of the time away from your regular workouts, pay attention to a few away-from-home details and you'll be set.

NUTRITION, SUPPLEMENTATION, AND WATER

For many people who travel—body-builders included—sound nutritional habits go out the door. The convenience and speed of stopping at a fast-food restaurant for a burger and fries make it enticing indeed. Business lunches are seldom designed for physique enhancement.

However, you can still salvage a nutritional meal while eating quickly and cheaply. Simply order

healthy salads—with low-calorie dressing, of course! Most of these salads will give you a nice ratio of high carbohydrates, moderate protein (you may want to supplement with aminos), and low fat.

When eating out, have your food grilled or baked—never fried—and ask for your fish, baked potato, or rice to be served dry. Always request that your salad dressing be served on the side.

I suggest packing extra supplements when you travel. Many times, you may not be able to eat all the various kinds of healthy foods you want. That's not an excuse to avoid getting the nutrients your body needs. Take extra supplements—especially aminos and vitamin C—when you feel the need.

Without a doubt, dehydration is a major obstacle for travelers. Think about it: how many times have you been on vacation, got caught up in all the business, and at the end of the day realized that you hardly drank any water?

The sure cure is to take a portable water bottle with you, keep it regularly filled, and drink from it often. Try to get at least 10 eight-ounce glasses of water throughout the day. When you're unable to drink water, drink juice. And eliminate or limit your caffeine and alcohol intake.

TRAINING

Working out on the road presents special challenges. Number one: finding a gym. Number two: finding equipment that you feel comfortable with. Let's face it—there's no place like your own gym, where you're comfortable with the atmosphere and equipment. And while a change of atmosphere can be inspiring, you may wish to just go through a lighter whole-body workout on the road. Save those hard and heavy workouts for when you get home.

You can get great workouts even if you're stuck in a hotel. Try push-ups (with various hand spacings to hit your chest and triceps), crunches for abs, chair curls for biceps, and suitcase rows for back; and you can briskly walk or run up the stairs for legs and cardiovascular work. You'll be amazed at how these simple exercises will maintain your muscle size and tone. Don't freak out if you can't find the time or a gym. After all, working out on the road isn't something you'll be doing for a year.

REST

As a rule, those who travel stay up late. And while having a great time into the wee hours is fun, it can take its toll—especially if you're not getting enough rest. Your body needs a certain number of hours of sleep each night to repair itself and grow. When you cut into those sleep hours, you're taking away from the maximum gains that your body could be making. Is night after night of late-night partying worth all that?

VISUALIZATION

Many of the top bodybuilding and fitness champions use vacation time as visualization time. Being away from your familiar surroundings allows you to think more creatively about your workouts, not to mention the rest of your life! New vistas open up in your mind as to how to make your workouts better and more effective and the rest of your life more rewarding and enjoyable. Being away from it all allows you to map out your workout strategy for the coming months.

KEEP EVERYTHING CONSISTENT

You will get so much more out of your time away from home if you stay on a regular eating, sleeping, drinking, supplementing, and training schedule. If you're on vacation, remember that vacations are designed for you to have fun. So have fun and enjoy a modified version of your healthy fitness lifestyle. If you're on a business trip, you'll function more effectively if you stick with fitness basics, rather than becoming overstressed, overtired, and overfed.

"You experience in your life whatever it is you're deeply convinced is true. If much of your thinking is about what you don't have, who you're not, what you can't have, and that you're a bad person, you'll continue to create the conditions in your life that make those thoughts come true."

It all goes back to that servant you carry in your head called your mind. That loyal and faithful servant will bring you whatever you deeply believe you deserve. First of all, let's get something straight: you're not a bad person; you're not someone who can't have a great body, lots of money, fame, fortune, happiness, or anything else in life, unless you've accepted the lie that you can't. Know the truth and let it set you free. A great body is yours, and so is anything else. Just believe it and get off your butt and go for it!

44

So You're a Beginner . . . Again!

Coming Back After a Layoff

Can I let you in on a little secret? At some point in your training, you're bound to experience a layoff. "No way," you say. "My training comes first—before anything!" Hey, at one time most of us believed that. However, sometimes injuries, work, school, family, vacations, training burnout, or the like can force a layoff. And you know what? That's okay. *The most important thing to remember is that a layoff is never permanent unless you want it to be. In fact, a training layoff can be an extremely valuable learning experience.*

The smart bodybuilder will take a training layoff of a few days to one week even when her training is going great. I want you to take a week off from training for every six to eight weeks of regular training. Why wait for the body to burn out or become injured when you can prevent it with a simple few days off at regular intervals?

So how do you get back into training if you've been away from the iron for a week or month or even a few years? Obviously, the length of layoff determines the speed with which you should come back. Someone who has

been regularly training hard and takes a week off can come back stronger and well-rested. Yet if you've been away from the iron for a few years, there are some things you should prepare for so you can avoid injury and burnout and get the maximum benefits from your training.

DON'T OVERDO IT

Doing too much too soon is the biggest cause of training injury and burnout. The unbridled passion for blasting the body just like in the "old days" is a huge reason why so many bodybuilders who have come back into the gym quit.

Allow your body plenty of time to come back slowly from a layoff. And while at first you may not be as strong as you were, don't worry—the body responds very quickly to training. Slow and steady is the key.

START WITH THE BASICS

I've seen too many bodybuilders come back from a long layoff and do supersets, tri-sets, forced reps, negatives, and the like—and this is during their first week! Don't you dare! Remember: start slowly and get your body accustomed to feeling the iron again. Stick to the basic exercises, and use freeweights.

Barbells and dumbbells will allow you to get back into the exercise groove naturally. They let your body do the basic exercises in the groove that feels most comfortable. Be patient. There'll be plenty of time for all those high-intensity principles later.

FIND THE GROOVE

Barbells and dumbbells are still the best vehicles for doing exercises in the greatest range of motion. Machines are good, but they operate in a fixed plane of motion. Your goal at this point is to rechannel those central nervous system muscle grooves that haven't been used for heavens knows how long.

TIME FOR RE-EVALUATION

A layoff is a great time to look at your old training program and goals and decide whether they really are what you want at this point in your life. Do you still have the time or inclination to pound your body with those heavy ballistic movements, or would you rather go for a more balanced approach that includes lighter weights and more cardiovascular training?

Look at your training goals and be realistic. Do you have the time to train like you used to? Do you want to train like you used to? Injuries are one of the main reasons people change their training programs and goals. Don't let it happen to you. Decide beforehand what kind of training program is important to you, then do it!

SET SHORT-TERM TRAINING GOALS

Be patient. Yeah, I know you've heard that many times, but it's true. Your body will get in great shape *if* you give it enough time. Look at your long-term physique and training goals, and break them into smaller bite-sized pieces.

Let's say that you want to lose 20 pounds; not 20 pounds of weight, but 20 pounds of fat. There's a big difference! Realistically, a fat loss of 0.5 to 1 pound a week is ideal. Ideal because it's not only healthy for your body, but you'll have the greatest chances of keeping the fat off if you do it slowly.

That's four pounds of *fat*—not water weight—lost in a month; and in 20 weeks, the entire 20 pounds can be burned up. It may not seem like much, but go to a grocery store and look at how big a four-pound piece of meat is. My friend, you'll then realize that four pounds of fat is a lot!

Focusing too much on the big goal is what stops most bodybuilders from reaching their goals. A journey of a thousand miles begins with a single step. The fun isn't so much in reaching the goal as it is the journey of working toward it. Set realistic goals, break those goals down into small components, and you'll achieve one goal after another.

TRY NEW THINGS

Boring people lead boring lives. Those who don't change anything in their lives—especially their training—stagnate and never grow. Hey, the law of nature is that either you grow or you die—there's no in-between!

Be open to new training techniques, routines, and anything else that can benefit you. Let your mind become, like the great martial artist Bruce Lee used to say, "formless, like water."

Throw away the misconception that there's only one way to train, get stronger, and grow. It simply isn't so. We are all very different in how our bodies respond to training. Find what's best for your body, then do it.

TAKE A BREAK

Give your body a forced rest, even if you're making great progress. I suggest taking an extra day or two off from training every three to four weeks. Then take a complete week off from training once every two months.

What bodybuilders are finding out is that it's not how long you stay in the gym that brings results, it's what you do while you're there. Forget those two- and three-hour marathon sessions. The sure formula for workout success is to make your workouts very brief, yet very intense.

Exercise intensity is what produces results—not length of time in the gym. Cut your number of sets in half and raise your intensity. If you're training hard, your workout per body part should last no longer than 30 minutes! Remember: you stimulate growth in the gym, but you grow outside the gym.

ENJOY EVERY WORKOUT

Why do people work out day after day when they don't really enjoy what they're doing? To me, that doesn't make sense. It's a waste of life and a huge waste of time. Working out isn't some kind of punishment that you must undergo to look and feel great.

If you don't enjoy doing a certain exercise or routine, then don't do it! Find those exercises and routines that you enjoy and give them everything you've got. You'll definitely make the best progress that way.

45

Working Around Injuries

When You've Got the Will, There's a Way to Keep Training When Hurting

Some years ago, I was talking with a friend in the gym about training. While the exercises he was doing didn't seem that peculiar, his responses did.

"So how's the training going?" I asked.

"Oh, pretty good, I guess, except for my shoulders," he replied.

"What's the problem?"

"They hurt like heck every time I do seated barbell behind-neck presses."

"So are you still doing them?"

"Yeah," he said. "I'm afraid to quit. My shoulders would lose too much size and strength."

My friend failed to realize that even though he was maintaining his size and strength, though only temporarily, the injury he was inflicting upon his shoulders would soon force him to stop training—possibly for good!

One of the primary elements of successful bodybuilding is the ability to train injury-free over a consistently long period. That means listening very carefully to your body when you feel any unusual aches or pains, and giving the injured body part plenty of time for repair and recuperation.

BUT I WANT TO TRAIN!

If you use your head and carefully choose your exercises, training with an injury won't be a problem. Erase those faulty misconceptions that you must constantly go heavy to get great results. It's simply not true.

The chart below lists some excellent exercises that can be substituted for movements that may be causing you pain.

Body part	Painful exercise	Substitute with
Shoulders	Press	Side lateral
Chest	Barbell bench press	Dumbbell incline press
Back	Chin-up	Reverse-grip pulldown
Triceps	French press	Dumbbell kickback
Biceps	Barbell curl	Ez-bar preacher curl
Quads	Squat	Leg press
Hamstrings	Leg curl	Stiff-legged deadlift (50 to 70% range of motion)
Calves	Standing calf raise	Toe raise on leg press machine

KEEPING UP THE INTENSITY

You can do plenty to up the intensity level of your workouts while an injured body part is healing. Once you've found the exercises that you're able to perform pain-free, apply the following Weider principles and watch what happens!

Supersets and Giant Sets

When you do two exercises back-to-back with little or no rest, you've done a superset. This is when you do one exercise each for opposing body parts, such as triceps and biceps.

In a giant set, you do four exercises back-to-back for the same body part. The key to getting the most from supersets and giant sets is to keep the rest between exercises to a minimum. This keeps the intensity level high to stimulate growth and strength.

Pre-Exhaustion

Pre-exhaustion fatigues a larger muscle group with an isolation movement so you'll be able to work it to exhaustion in a subsequent compound movement. Otherwise, you're limited by a smaller muscle group tiring too soon—before the larger muscles have worked enough.

For example, take the chest—a big muscle group—and the triceps—a small muscle group. Your chest muscles are far more powerful than your triceps, which usually fatigue long before the chest does. The solution to getting maximum chest stimulation is pre-exhaustion.

For instance, first do a set of pec deck flyes, and then immediately do a set of dumbbell incline presses. This should allow your chest muscles to fatigue at about the same rate as your triceps.

Partial Reps

Partial reps are just that—working your muscles in only their strongest range of motion (rather than the full range of motion in a complete rep). Partials allow you to handle heavy weight for growth and strength. To do partials, simply take a good basic exercise and move the weight through only the part of the movement where you're at your strongest. Then lock out the weight to full muscle contraction.

Only a few inches of movement is needed to really get those muscles burning. Partials might be the solution you need to overload your muscles without overstressing an injured body part.

As with any exercise and training program, you've got to do a little homework and find the exercises you can handle during injury rehabilitation. In a perfect world, we'd never get injured—but things do go wrong, even when we're careful. The good news is that the body will heal itself if we give it the rest it needs.

Use good form on every exercise and be careful when you train. If you train safely, you should be able to enjoy the incredible benefits of the bodybuilding lifestyle for many years to come.

"It is the young man of little faith who says, 'I am nothing.' It is the young man of true conception who says, 'I am everything,' and then goes to prove it."

–Edward W. Bok

My friend, you need to know that those with big faith get big results. People with little faith get little results. When you have big faith in yourself, you easily believe that a great body and anything else in life can be yours without an ounce of doubt. The more faith you have, the more possibilities open up to you. Faith is like a big door that's waiting to be opened—and behind that door are incredible things for you to experience. Just have faith in your abilities and believe in great things, and feel what it would be like to experience all those things. You can have them, and much sooner than you ever dreamed possible. Friend, what I'm telling you is absolutely as true as this book you're holding in your hands and the words you're now reading.

46

The Perfect Balance

Now Is the Time to Make Your Fitness Goals a Reality

Think how easy your life would be if someone handed you a piece of paper with instructions on how and when to train, the amount and types of cardio work you should do, proven strategies for dietary success, tips on how to avoid psychological roadblocks, and practical advice on recovery. Well, this is that piece of paper! It's time to make your training productive and your fitness goals a reality.

DIET

- Eat four to six small meals a day spaced about three hours apart.
- Make each meal consist of 50 percent carbs (rice, whole grains, pasta, green vegetables, potatoes, yams, fruit); 35 percent protein (chicken, fish, turkey, eggwhites, protein powder, lean beef); and 15 percent fat.
- Drink at least 80 ounces (10 glasses) of water per day, no exceptions!
- Take a good multivitamin/mineral supplement every day and 1,000 mg

of vitamin C three times per day (at breakfast, lunch, and dinner for a daily total of 3,000 mg).

WEIGHT TRAINING

There are lots of great training routines you can do, depending on your fitness goals. Here are some basic guidelines you can use regardless of which routine you choose.

- Avoid overtraining. If you feel sore or tired from your last workout and it's time to train again, take an extra day or two off.
- Get in and get out. Keep your training intensity high by keeping your rest between sets and exercises to a minimum. Take only enough rest between sets to catch your breath. Take only a few minutes of rest between body parts.
- Change your exercises, sets, rest, reps, and weights often. *I suggest that every workout you do something different.* This helps keep your workouts fresh and enjoyable, and prevents boredom and burnout.

CARDIOVASCULAR TRAINING

Some people claim that you must do cardiovascular work for 45 minutes a day and sweat like a hog. Based on information I've received from the pros I've interviewed, people I've put on programs, and my own experience, I disagree. We've found that if you do it correctly, you can get great results with as little as 21 minutes per cardio workout, three times per week. Here's a great cardio routine that makes use of the treadmill.

1. Start with the treadmill at 3.3 to 4.2 mph (depending upon your age and fitness level). Keep the incline at 0 for five minutes.
2. On minute 6, raise the incline to 10 percent.
3. On minute 18, lower the incline to 5 percent.
4. On minute 19, lower the incline to 0 and maintain through minute 21, after which you're finished.
5. Be sure to move your arms way out in front of and behind as you walk, and take long strides on the treadmill.
6. Don't hold onto the side handles or the front of the machine. Make your legs do the work. Don't cheat and try to make it easier on yourself. You're only robbing yourself of the benefits.
7. Keep your aerobic work in your target heart rate range (take 220 minus your age, then multiply that number by 60 to 70 percent) for no less than 15 minutes.

MENTAL TRAINING

- Keep your mind firmly fixed on the body you want.
- Visualize the details of that body's look.
- Vividly imagine how you would feel with your new body.

- Accept the idea that you have your new body right now—not just someday. See it, feel it, and believe that it's happening to you now!
- Consider every exercise you do, every bit of food you eat, and everything you drink, with the question: *Is this helping me or holding me back in my fitness goals?*
- Set big goals, but use small ones as stepping stones.
- Be patient and never quit. You will never achieve your fitness goals if you quit. Live by the motto *Starting means I'm half-finished.*

RECOVERY

- Get to the gym. Work out briefly, but intensely. Then get out and grow. So many people complain that their routines aren't working. The biggest problem is that they are overtrained and under-rested.
- Your body needs time to recuperate and repair itself from your workouts. Listen to your body. If you're still sore or tired from your last workout, forget about going to the gym, even if it's your scheduled day to train.
- Whenever feasible, get a full-body massage. Massage not only feels incredible, it has many therapeutic benefits: it speeds healing, promotes blood flow, and increases range of motion, for example.
- Always warm up before each workout. Be sure each body part is fully warmed up before using heavy weight. *And if you ever feel a slight twinge or unusual pain, immediately stop that exercise and switch to one that causes no pain.* Never, never, continue to exercise when you are in pain. Seek professional care. Your goal should be to enjoy the benefits of working out for many, many years.

PART VII

All the Answers You Need

47

Answers to Your Most-Asked Questions

I have a question. Why aren't you asking more questions? About bodybuilding, that is. Questions give you the answers to problems. Whatever training problem you're now having, someone had the same problem before and found the solution.

Still, something keeps people from asking questions. Is it fear? Pride? How can you learn if you don't ask? Someone once said that you can't live long enough to make all the mistakes yourself, so you should study the lives of others. Let's begin by eliminating 10 of those possible training mistakes.

Which supplements should I take?

A good start is a multivitamin/mineral supplement, which you should take right after breakfast and another after dinner. Next, I recommend a high-quality protein powder derived from whey, egg, or milk and egg. Building muscle requires additional protein, so you must ensure that your body is getting sufficient nourishment.

You might want to try a creatine monohydrate supplement. In some people, regular use of creatine monohydrate helps increase energy for training, which means you can train harder—but not longer—for increased intensity and better results. Like all supplements, always follow label directions.

I'm getting bored with my routine. How do I change it to keep it fresh and productive?

The process is more involved than simply doing something different the next time you go into the gym. Here's a better approach. Experiment with a variety of exercises until you find at least five exercises for each body part that give you good results. Each time you work out, pick two or three and do them.

In addition, don't be afraid to change the *order* in which you train. For example, in your chest workout, if you're doing incline barbell presses, decline presses, and flyes, try reversing the order. Change rep speed, workout tempo, take an extra rest day, pile on more weights. Just play around with as many variables as possible, and keep your body always wondering what you're going to make it do next!

I get conflicting advice about how much cardiovascular training I should be doing. What's best?

Start with your goals. If you're training for an endurance activity like a marathon, then spending more time on aerobic training makes sense. If you want to pack on mass but still keep your midsection nice and tight, then shoot for 20 to 30 minutes of cardio training three times a week. If you're lifting heavy; training intensely; resting no longer than 45 seconds between sets (but longer for heavy multijoint movements); and eating a lowfat diet with lots of complex carbs and protein, this cardio plan should work well.

In order of training importance, how would you rank heavy weights, form, and intensity?

You asked for it, so here's how I rank them:

- **Form**—To develop maximum size and strength with minimum risk of injury, excellent form is foremost. Strict exercise form makes muscles work harder and forces them to respond by growing stronger much more rapidly.
- **Intensity**—Many would rank heavy weights second, but you can increase workout intensity in a number of ways other than using heavy weights. Intensity is the degree to which you make your muscles work. Nothing secret here. If you raise your training intensity, you automatically increase your results.

- **Heavy weights**—Where would bodybuilders who want serious results be without them? Bodybuilding is based on progressive resistance, which means progressively lifting heavier weights. Look at the muscle size you have now. You will not get any bigger unless you add intensity, and one way to do that is with progressively heavier weights.

A few guys in the gym have taken steroids and have really grown. What are the risks involved?

When it comes to steroids, most people see only the big muscles. But for every big guy or gal you see who has spent major dollars for a drug-induced "growth" cycle (which is commonly accompanied by water retention, a bad attitude called *roid rage*, and zits), several others are duped into buying counterfeit steroids.

The market is flooded with fake stuff, which, at about $150 for 10cc, is very expensive cooking oil. Since you don't really know what the counterfeiters are loading into the vials, you're playing Russian roulette. Steroids destroy real bodybuilding. Most people come to the sport to look and feel good. I believe the majority of people who've experimented with steroids do so for the following reasons:

- They aren't willing to invest the time, discipline, or commitment to explore *every* conceivable routine that could work for them.

- They aren't willing to lift heavy, train intensely, supplement wisely, eat nutritiously, and get the proper amount of sleep—the things it takes to grow big and strong without chemicals.
- They have little concern for the future of their health, the direction of their lives, or the sport of bodybuilding. They live and burn out by the motto "I want it now."
- They are easily swayed by what "those in the know" say they must do to succeed.

They are sheep and will never be leaders or what we once called heroes. How can they be, if their muscle, strength, and training programs come from a pill or out of a vial? Bottom line: you don't need drugs!

I want to gain muscle mass. What kinds of foods should I eat?

A 400-pound tuna! Seriously, big muscles need protein. How much? Figure on 0.7 to 1.3 grams of protein per pound of body weight. For most people, eating that much protein throughout the day can be difficult unless they bolster one or two of their meals with a high-quality protein supplement. Get the rest of your protein from sources like eggwhites, lean beef, skinless chicken and turkey, and nonfat dairy products.

The quality of your carbs is also important. Carbs not only give you energy, but spare protein from being burned for fuel as well. Great carb sources include fresh vegetables, rice, whole grains, lentils, beans, and fruits.

Eat four or more small meals throughout the day. You must keep your body continually supplied with nutrients. Drink lots of water, also, to keep the body well hydrated. And get plenty of sleep. If you're serious about

packing on more size, don't party it up, or exhaustion will stall your progress.

I train very hard, yet I'm barely making any size or strength gains. What's wrong?

And I thought you'd be happy with two inches on your arms in seven days. It really sounds like your body is telling you it needs something different. How about taking a week off from training or trying a new workout? For the natural bodybuilder, frequently changing workouts is a must!

Just how often should you change? Many bodybuilders get excellent results by doing something different every time they work out. And it doesn't have to be a drastic change. Just altering the amount of weight used, rest between sets, the number of reps, grip, body angle, or the order of exercises can make a huge difference. Use your head and think up new routines that would be fun. Then do them!

I see so many products advertised as the number-one supplement or a training system promising quick gains. How can I tell what works and what's hype?

Welcome to the circus and all the smoke and mirrors. Understand this: the majority of those shapely spokespersons you see in ads built their great bodies with years of intense weight workouts using the basic movements. Product manufacturers go to those people because they look great and can aid them in their sales goals. They are hired to sell product. Always keep that in mind.

Don't go ga-ga over every before and after picture you see in the ads. You'd be surprised at what the right lighting, a good tan, the right posing angle, tailored clothing, and 60 days of strict dieting can do to an out-of-shape but previously weight-trained physique.

The most reputable companies will have legitimate, objective, and independent scientific studies that demonstrate the efficacy of their supplement or training system. If they don't, stay away from them.

Ask yourself: just who are these experts who are selling or endorsing the product? What are their real credentials? Read between the lines. Write these companies and request an assay of their product. Study the list of ingredients minus all the fancy terminology to find out what's really inside.

You'd be amazed at how companies can "invent the truth" based on slick ads, testimonials, and public relations. The bodybuilding community needs to clean house and weed out the unscrupulous ones and make the other companies hold themselves up to a higher standard. Let the buyer beware, however—it all begins with you and your wallet!

I'm a confused beginner. With so much bodybuilding and fitness information available in the magazines each month, how do I know which training program to follow?

Talk about confusion! With so many advertisements relying on so-called experts to sell you "guaranteed" training systems or "better" supplements, who do you believe? Read relevant articles and use that knowledge to make informed decisions when considering a purchase. Ask yourself if what the author is saying is important to helping you achieve your immediate and long-term goals. Goals change, so don't hang on to those things that aren't in perfect harmony with whatever goals you presently have.

How important are genes to bodybuilding success?

If you're a competitive bodybuilder or want to be, genetics is of paramount importance. Those blessed with good genetics gain size and strength quickly and have an inherent muscle structure and look that is very appealing.

But let's define bodybuilding success. For the vast majority who don't compete and don't want to, genetics can be overrated. You can be young or old, fat or thin, tall or short; but if you follow the basic bodybuilding principles, you will succeed in improving your physique—a lot! No doubt about it.

"Take care of the inside, and the outside will take care of itself."

You are a mind with a body. An old sage once said, "Your body was designed to carry your mind; not the other way around." Here's a little something else for you to ponder. Your body can't think; it only responds to the commands given to it by your mind! Does your body tell your mind when to breathe? No. Does your body tell your mind when and how to heal a cut? No. Your mind is the command center for everything that happens to your body. Yet most people still believe that fixing the outside first will change the inside. Look at the way you look. *You have the body you now have because that's exactly the body you believe you should have.* It fits your picture of the body and performance level you've accepted for yourself to have. It can be no different until you *first* change the picture in your mind (inside) of how your body should look and feel. For most people, and hopefully you, that's an uncomfortable thought. Why on earth would you choose to look like this when for so long you've told everyone and even yourself that you want to look and feel better? Again, give your mind a new picture to work on, and it will show you the ways in which you can achieve it! Any kind of long-term and lasting change must first come from the inside. See and believe in yourself as a smarter, more energetic, healthier, dynamic, enthusiastic, and incredibly blessed and successful person, and you will become that person in a very short time. But first you must change the inside—and as you do, the outside will take care of itself!

More Answers to Common Bodybuilding Questions

Questions. For the smart bodybuilder, they're the keys that open the door to greater knowledge and results. The better the question, the more complete the answer. A thirst for knowledge can help propel you to your bodybuilding and fitness goals. I've put together a list of a few more of the bodybuilding questions I am asked most frequently, along with their answers.

How often should I change my program?

Some pros will change their routine every workout. This is the essence of instinctive training. Many other bodybuilding stars and experts will stay with the same program for up to three months. I know of many others who have found a group of exercises that work extremely well for them all the time. They include these exercises in every workout for those particular body parts.

Once you feel bored or you're not getting the results you seek, make a slight change in your program. Many times, that is all that's needed to get you growing.

When should I go up in weight?

As a rule of thumb, whenever you're able to do 10 fairly easy reps on any exercise, go up in weight. Small-increment increases are the best to ensure that muscles and connective tissue will grow and get stronger. A weight increase of 10 percent a week would be very good. However, if you're not able to do that each week, don't be discouraged. The most important thing is to go up in weight—if only slightly—as often as possible.

On each workout, should I do each exercise one time for my entire body before doing my second set?

Many beginning bodybuilders are put on this circuit type of training where one set per body part is done before moving to the next body part exercise. For the serious bodybuilder, however, the best results in mass and strength are obtained when all exercises for a body part are completed before moving to the next body part in the workout.

Is muscle soreness bad?

Many bodybuilders welcome a slight muscle soreness as a sign that they worked their muscles hard. However, a very deep and severe soreness probably means that you did too much; you should take it easy and give your body a chance to heal and recover. Don't train that body part again until all soreness is gone.

I train hard but I can't gain any size. Why?

There could be many reasons. First of all, look at your training intensity. Are you working out hard enough? I didn't say *long enough*, but *hard enough*. Most people train too long and do too much, and that leads to overtraining. Cut back on the amount of work you do in the gym, and raise your intensity level.

Be sure you're getting enough nutrients and that your diet is good. To gain size, you should be ingesting about 1 gram of protein per pound of body weight daily. Keep your stress level low, and be sure to get enough rest. Get seven and one-half to nine hours of sleep each night.

And by all means, don't work out if the body part you're scheduled to train is still sore from your last workout. You've got to let the body rest and recuperate completely if you expect to grow and get stronger.

I want to train, but I feel tired with little energy. What's wrong?

You may not be getting enough carbohydrates, the most readily available fuel for the body. You get carbs from fruit, vegetables, rice, grains, and pasta. Keep your intake of complex carbohydrates (rice, potatoes, vegetables, pasta, grains) moderate to high, because this source of fuel is long-burning. Be sure to eat four to six small meals each day spaced every two to three hours apart. Also, drink at least 10 eight-ounce glasses of water a day.

What are the best exercises for mass?

The basics. If you want size and strength, you must do plenty of the following: squats for thighs; donkey raises for calves; deadlifts for hamstrings, low back, and traps; bench presses for chest; barbell or dumbbell presses for shoulders; dumbbell or EZ-bar French presses for triceps; and barbell curls for biceps.

What are the best exercises for big arms?

For big biceps, you can't beat heavy barbell and dumbbell curls. For big triceps, close-grip bench presses, dips, and French presses are king-size arm builders.

How often should I train?

It all depends on your level of development. Beginners who have less than nine months in weight training can make great progress working the whole body three times per week (such as Monday, Wednesday, and Friday).

Advanced bodybuilders (those with more than nine months training) can make excellent progress by using the split training system. In this system you train your entire body twice per week. A typical split system workout would be upper body on Monday and Thursday, lower body on Tuesday and Friday. You would rest on Wednesday, Saturday, and Sunday.

How long should my workouts last?

If your workouts (for one to two body parts) take longer than 45 minutes, you're spending too much time in the gym. Remember, it's not how long you stay, it's what you do while you're there.

You don't need to do a lot of exercises or sets and reps to make your body grow. Experiment and find the number of exercises, sets, and reps that work best for you, and stick with them.

"Don't believe you're traveling down the right road just because everyone else is too."

Wow, how true is that? We like to think we're on the road to health and prosperity and every other good thing in life because it's the road so many others are traveling—but is it? For the most part, it's not. The majority of people have found the well-worn path, and to them that's become the only way to the things in life they say they want. Too bad it rarely leads them there. Find your own path, and don't you dare be afraid to follow it. Go the opposite direction of the crowd. You're not a sheep, and you don't need a shepherd to tell you which direction you must go to build your body or do anything else you want in life. Listen to your conscience and your heart, and you won't go wrong.

Index

Weights
  for beginners, 6
  for intermediate bodybuilders,
    46–47
Wolff, Robert, vii, ix
Workouts
  advanced, 94–96
  for beginners, 11–13
  defined, 5

for intermediate bodybuilders,
  44–46
length of, 223
Wraps, 82
Wrist curls, 65–66

Z
Zane, Frank, 120
Zottman curls, 180–82